MEDIATION:
A PRACTICAL GUIDE
FOR LAWYERS

Second Edition

MARJORIE MANTLE, LL.B.

Founder, Mediation Scotland;
Honorary Lecturer,
University of Dundee Law School

EDINBURGH
University Press

Edinburgh University Press is one of the leading university presses in the UK. We publish academic books and journals in our selected subject areas across the humanities and social sciences, combining cutting-edge scholarship with high editorial and production values to produce academic works of lasting importance. For more information visit our website: edinburghuniversitypress.com

© Marjorie Mantle, 2017

First edition published by Dundee University Press in 2011

Edinburgh University Press Ltd
The Tun – Holyrood Road
12 (2f) Jackson's Entry
Edinburgh EH8 8PJ

Typeset in 10/13 Adobe Sabon by
IDSUK (DataConnection) Ltd, and
printed and bound in Great Britain by
CPI Group (UK) Ltd, Croydon CR0 4YY

A CIP record for this book is available from the British Library

ISBN 978 1 4744 2025 9 (paperback)
ISBN 978 1 4744 2026 6 (webready PDF)
ISBN 978 1 4744 2027 3 (epub)

The right of Marjorie Mantle to be identified as author of this work has been asserted in accordance with the Copyright, Designs and Patents Act 1988 and the Copyright and Related Rights Regulations 2003 (SI No. 2498).

CONTENTS

Appendices

TABLE OF CASES

TABLE OF LEGISLATION

INTRODUCTION

In his opening address to the Global Pound Conference in Singapore in March 2016, The Honourable the Chief Justice Sundaresh Menon spoke of a

> growing recognition that access to justice can take place outside the courtroom. Gone are the days when disputants believed that their quest for justice could only be pursued in courtrooms. Increasingly, disputants look beyond the traditional court-based approaches to resolve their disputes.[1]

Menon CJ goes on to discuss how increasing globalisation, cross-border trade and labour movement lead inevitably to disputes which may need multiple legal systems for resolution. He highlights mediation as being a viable alternative to the traditional court processes, and acknowledges:

> The benefits of mediation have come to be appreciated across the board from family or matrimonial disputes to business partnerships and commercial relationships. This is a trend that appears to be gaining momentum and we should encourage this.[2]

The statements of Menon CJ echo comments made by the Court of Appeal in Ireland in *Ryan* v *Walls Construction Ltd*:

> As already pointed out mediation is now firmly established as a well-respected alternative dispute resolution process. Whilst it is not a panacea, it has proven to be very beneficial and it has succeeded in bringing about settlements of seemingly intractable disputes. Experience teaches that even if the mediation itself is unsuccessful it frequently succeeds in dealing with some of the issues in dispute or creates a climate for continued negotiation.[3]

It is difficult to find out how many mediations take place around the world. However, in Scotland a review of civil justice statistics for 2014–15 suggested that the use of alternative dispute resolution may affect the number of cases initiated in court. 'The reasons behind this decrease [in the number of cases over the past three years] are not known but possible factors include increasing use of alternative methods of dispute resolution and concern over costs for litigants should they lose the case.'[4]

As I wrote in the first edition of this book, you may, as a lawyer, have had limited exposure to mediation as a form of dispute resolution. This book is a tool to help you understand mediation, and how it can benefit you and your clients. Many a time, a party or a lawyer has told me that they have 'already tried to mediate and it didn't work'. On digging a little deeper I find that the 'mediation' has been people shouting at each other down the phone, exchanging terse correspondence, or sticking dogmatically to their point of view. As Nancy Rogers and Roger Salem note, 'Mediation is usually a by-product of failure – the inability of disputants to work out their own differences. Each party typically comes to mediation locked into a position that the other(s) will not accept.'[5]

If you are not familiar with mediation as a form of dispute resolution, it may not be easy for you to consider whether it is appropriate to broach it as an option with your clients. This uncertainty could hamper your duty to serve the best interests of your clients, or lead you ultimately to lose their custom as they take their legal business elsewhere. Even if you do have theoretical knowledge of mediation, you may be finding it difficult to use it in a way which benefits your clients. This book is intended as a mediation handbook and guide for lawyers. It provides you with information, tips, checklists, sample documents and case studies. It aims to be practical, with some academic parts added for your interest.

Since writing the first edition, I have been heartened to see the growth in the use of mediation and its increasing acceptance by courts and legislatures around the world. To evidence this, I have included information referring to North America, the Asia-Pacific region, some recent case law and new legislation. I have also added a section about online dispute resolution, which is growing in importance. The examples of disputes which I use are deliberately simple. The point of this book is not to delve into the intricacies of complex matters, but rather to provide you with examples of mediation in practice.

Of course, many mediations are about highly complex issues. A number of parties may be involved, and the stakes may be high. In mediation, the opportunity is there to listen, to sort out what is key to each party, and to develop workable solutions for all. It works for big business, public authorities, families, neighbours and business colleagues. As a Sheriff in Edinburgh Sheriff Court wrote:

> Many cases are raised particularly as Small Claims or Summary Causes because of Parties' feelings that they have suffered some injustice, such as in consumer contracts. Some of these cases raise more complex legal problems than anticipated although the reason for the raising of the action seems straightforward. A judicial disposal dealing with the legal point may leave Parties feeling that the system is unjust.
>
> Mediation offers an alternative allowing Parties in such cases to reach a resolution that is acceptable to both of them. Mediation is not suitable in all disputes, nor always successful, but where it is thought to be suitable, it is worth attempting. It would be a retrograde step if the process were not to continue. It is a process which appears to work best in conjunction with the court process.[6]

I agree with all he says, except the last sentence. As well as working well with the court process, mediation is an ideal stand-alone option in appropriate situations. This book reflects my experience as a mediator, as a business person and as an academic. There are bound to be parts with which other mediators disagree. That's fine, as flexibility is one of the great things about mediation. There are some 'rules', but the process is robust enough to adjust to individual disputes and personalities.

I hope you find this book enjoyable to read and a useful guide.

Notes

1. Menon, *Shaping the Future*, para. 16.
2. Ibid., para. 19.
3. *Ryan*, para. 53.
4. Scottish Government, *Civil Justice Statistics*, p. 4. (See also interesting work undertaken by Law Business Research Ltd.)
5. Rogers and Salem 1993: 7.
6. Report of Edinburgh Sheriff Court Mediation Service, 2006.

Chapter 1

WHAT IS MEDIATION?

There are many definitions of mediation, but in essence they all convey the following message: 'Mediation is an opportunity to resolve a dispute without resorting to formal procedures such as court. The process is usually voluntary and is facilitated by an independent third party whose role is to help the parties develop solutions in a confidential environment.'

Later in this book, I discuss why the elements of this definition matter for your work with your clients. For now, let's look at where mediation fits into dispute resolution options.

The options

Beneficial though mediation is, it may not always be the appropriate way to assist your clients. The spectrum of dispute resolution options ranges from the parties sorting things out themselves to an adjudicator making a decision in a formal setting. So where does mediation sit?

The least formal option is negotiation (Figure 1.1).

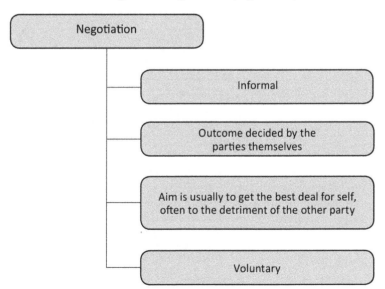

Negotiation

Informal

Outcome decided by the parties themselves

Aim is usually to get the best deal for self, often to the detriment of the other party

Voluntary

Figure 1.1   Negotiation

If we continue along the spectrum, the next option is mediation (Figure 1.2).

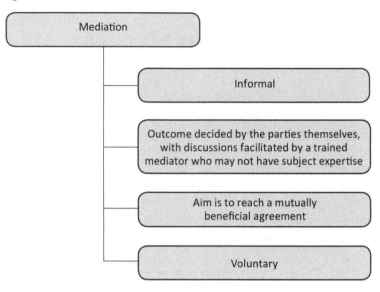

Figure 1.2   Mediation

Matters start to become more formal with arbitration (Figure 1.3).

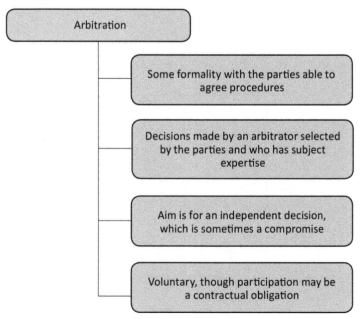

Figure 1.3   Arbitration

The far end of the spectrum is court or tribunal (Figure 1.4).

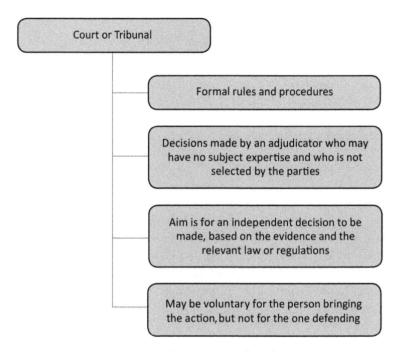

Figure 1.4   Court or tribunal

In 40-plus years in business and more latterly in mediation, I have seen many a dispute go directly from failure at the negotiation stage to formal proceedings being instigated. Positions become entrenched, delays occur, costs and stress levels rise, and by the time matters are resolved no party is completely happy. As one author points out:

> It seems obvious, but a frequently over-looked fact is that disputes end up before the courts because good lawyers are, not unreasonably, giving different advice. Mediation therefore is about finding an intelligent, pragmatic and commercial basis for resolving the dispute above and beyond the minutiae of legal argument.[1]

Mediation slots in as an option between negotiation and formal proceedings, so is an essential part of your toolkit for your discussions with clients. If you need more convincing of this, read on.

Why bother with mediation?

It may be tempting to consider mediation to be the last matter on your list of priorities. As you might expect, I suggest that you reconsider this approach, because of the following influences:

- Financial
- Competitive pressure
- Professional standards
- Access to justice
- International perspective

Let's look at each in turn.

Financial

Why miss an opportunity to increase your fee income? In a competitive market, lawyers who have different ways of helping their clients are the ones who have the best chance of increasing revenue. As long ago as 2009, Ian Hanger AM QC, in his address to the Asian Mediation Association conference, noted that many lawyers in Australia were earning significant income representing clients in mediation. Addressing the Faculty of Advocates in Edinburgh in the same year, Mr Hanger[2] reassured the audience that contrary to the myth, the initials 'ADR' do not stand for 'Alarming Drop in Revenue'. (Throughout this book, I use the abbreviation 'ADR' to mean 'Alternative Dispute Resolution', which has been the terminology for some time. However, some authors, and indeed Chief Justice Menon in his address[3] to the Global Pound Conference, use the term 'Appropriate Dispute Resolution'. The choice is yours.)

This is supported by research undertaken into the attitudes of construction lawyers to the use of mediation: 'many of the respondents also considered mediation as an opportunity to enhance their fee earning potential, with 78% strongly disagreeing that the growth of mediation would be detrimental to future earnings.' The report goes on to note that 'a large majority, 88%, strongly or somewhat agreed that mediation would provide lawyers with an opportunity to offer further services to their clients'.[4]

Tie this in with the attitude in the Western world, where we expect fast responses and resolutions. (Think how frustrating it is when your computer 'slows down'. It's probably taking only a few seconds longer than usual, but our expectations are that things should happen instantly.) Are you prepared to run the risk of losing business because you have not considered the possibility of mediation to achieve a speedy outcome? Clients are becoming more demanding and expecting faster results.

Sidebar

Where do new clients come from? While I have yet to discover any research into this, my experience of working with hundreds of small to medium sized businesses across various sectors is that the majority of new customers or clients come via word of mouth recommendations. So what has this got to do with mediation? Later in this book we will consider some of the benefits of mediation – one of them being that usually matters can be resolved more quickly than through the normal processes which potentially lead to protracted negotiations, court or tribunal hearings. If you want to grow your client base, then consider the following.

You work with a client over, say, three years to help resolve a complex issue. At the end of that time, the matter is sorted and your client is so delighted that he recommends you to two friends. Great – you have two new clients.

Let's say, though, that mediation is an appropriate option for this matter and everything is sorted out in six months. Again, your client is so delighted that he recommends you to two friends. Great – you have two new clients.

If you then work with these people in similar circumstances, look at the maths:

1. work with existing client for three years; at the end you have three clients – one old, two new
2. help an existing client using mediation over six months; at the end you have three clients – one old, two new
   a. after another six months you have nine clients – three 'old', six new – because each has recommended you to two people
   b. after another six months you have 27 clients – nine 'old', eighteen new
   c. after three years you have 729 clients

All right – I agree. There are no guarantees in this equation, but even if it's only half right your client base has grown substantially. My suggestion is that the appropriate use of mediation gives you the opportunity to increase your fee income through the client growth.

For further discussion about client profiles, see Appendix 12.

Competitive pressure

No matter what business you are in, there are always competitors ready to snatch your share of the market. The unwary ostriches find out too late that the world has moved on around them. Take, for example, the watch industry in Switzerland, which resolutely kept producing mechanical timepieces and failed to recognise the impact of quartz technology. The number of employees in the Swiss watch industry plunged from 90,000 in 1970 to around 30,000 in 1984.[5] Watches that no longer required a battery and had few moving parts could be produced more cheaply. Consequently, Switzerland's 50 per cent world market share was eroded by products from America and Japan. (In 1983, the Swiss industry's fortunes were revived with the development of the Swatch watch.)

Whether you are a sole practitioner or part of a large firm, you are aware of your competitors. If you work in the UK, where there is limited use of mediation at present, you may think there is no need for you to consider it. However, in his speech in Asia, Mr Hanger discussed the speed at which mediation was taken up by the profession, brought into legislation and incorporated into Court Rules in Australia. Over a ten-year period, the use of mediation moved from being considered a 'weak' option to one where some judges regard a lawyer's failure to discuss the availability and benefits of mediation as potentially negligent.

Professional standards

As you know, the profession sets conduct and service standards to which lawyers must adhere. Consider the following examples and how they impact on your duty to discuss mediation with your clients. (Other jurisdictions have similar standards.)

Scotland

Rule B1.9 of the Law Society of Scotland deals with effective communication. The guidance relating to this Rule deals directly with dispute resolution and incorporates the statement:

> Solicitors should have a sufficient understanding of commonly available alternative dispute resolution options to allow proper consideration and communication of options to a client in considering the client's interests and objectives.[6]

England and Wales

The Solicitors Regulation Authority's *Code of Conduct* states that a required outcome is that 'clients are in a position to make informed decisions about the services they need, how their matter will be handled and the options available to them'.[7]

Canada

The Model Code of Professional Conduct states at 3.2–4:

> A lawyer must advise and encourage a client to compromise or settle a dispute whenever it is possible to do so on a reasonable basis and must discourage the client from commencing or continuing useless legal proceedings.
>
> Commentary: A lawyer should consider the use of alternative dispute resolution (ADR) when appropriate, inform the client of ADR options and, if so instructed, take steps to pursue those options.[8]

If you fail to adhere to these standards, you run the risk of your client making a formal complaint against you. If the complaint is upheld, you may face the possibility of financial sanctions.

Access to justice

The title of Lord Woolf's report in 1996 brought the term 'access to justice' to the forefront. Subsequent changes to the Civil Procedures Rules and later Practice Directions address two aims of Lord Woolf's recommendations. As His Lordship says in his final report, these are

> that of encouraging the resolution of disputes before they come to litigation, for example by greater use of pre-litigation disclosure and of ADR, and that of encouraging settlement, for example by introducing plaintiffs' offers to settle, and by disposing of issues so as to narrow the dispute . . . although the primary role of the court is as a forum for deciding cases it is right that the court should encourage the parties to consider the use of ADR as a means to resolve their disputes . . .[9]

In Scotland, the report by The Right Honourable Lord Gill in 2009 echoed these sentiments, stating: 'It [ADR] is therefore a valuable complement to the work of the courts'.[10] The recommendation proposed that resources be developed to support the referral of suitable cases to ADR. In his preface to *A Guide to Mediating in Scotland*,

Lord Gill refers to a study trip to Maryland which he undertook in 2003. He says: 'That visit persuaded me of the value of mediation, not only as a means of diverting disputes from the courts but as a means of promoting amity in the resolution of them.'[11]

The principle of access to justice was one of the drivers in the development of the 2008 EU Directive for cross-border disputes in civil and commercial matters.[12] The preamble states:

> the establishment of basic principles in this area [alternative dispute resolution] is an essential step towards enabling the appropriate development and operation of extrajudicial procedures for the settlement of disputes in civil and commercial matters so as to simplify and improve access to justice.[13]

While not specifically mentioning the phrase 'access to justice', the 2013 EU Directive on alternative dispute resolution for consumer disputes refers to 'ensuring access to simple, efficient, fast and low-cost ways of resolving domestic and cross-border disputes'.[14] The Directive and Regulation (EU) No. 524/2013 provide for a mechanism for online dispute resolution (ODR) for consumer disputes. See Appendix 1 for more information about ODR.

Government has also recognised the importance of enabling access to justice for those requiring legal aid. For example, in England and Wales the Legal Aid, Sentencing and Punishment of Offenders Act 2012, when defining 'Civil Legal Services', refers to 'assistance and advice in the form of . . . mediation and other forms of dispute resolution'.[15]

International perspective

The time when it took months to find out what was happening in the rest of the world is long gone. Through the Internet we can readily see that many other countries have embraced the use of mediation. Legislation has been introduced to support it, law schools include it in the curriculum, and clients routinely expect to be offered it. We in the UK should not be left behind.

For your clients, one of the key benefits of the 2008 EU Directive is that it allows for written agreements made from mediation to be enforceable.[16] As the Green Paper[17] had recognised, there were differences among Member States regarding the enforcement of agreements reached through mediation.[18] Now, if your client reaches an agreement through mediation with a supplier in Germany, he will be able to enforce this more readily if necessary.

Other parts of the world have recognised the need for ADR options across different regions. For example, in recent years Singapore has taken great strides towards the use and development of mediation. (Rather confusingly, the names of its various organisations are fairly similar.) The Singapore Mediation Centre trains mediators in the region and undertakes mediations for domestic commercial disputes. The Singapore International Mediation Centre, as the name may suggest, has international mediators dealing with international commercial disputes. The Singapore International Mediation Institute, established in 2014, sets the professional standards for mediators and certifies competence. In addition, in his address to the Global Pound Conference, Menon CJ announced the launch of the Singapore International Dispute Resolution Academy (SIDRA), 'the first regional hub dedicated to training and educational excellence in negotiation and dispute resolution'. He goes on to say:

> Significantly, SIDRA will offer an international platform for exchanging and developing ideas on theory, practice and policy development and will bring a strong presence of contemporary Asian voices into the global conversations on dispute resolution.[19]

In my view, there seems to be no reason why other jurisdictions will not take a similar path in the future.

How do clients in other parts of the world use mediation? Lord Gill's report contains a brief summary of the use of mediation in other jurisdictions.[20] For a useful overview of the European position, see the Libralex publication from February 2016.[21]

Examples

1. In the USA, mediation has been undertaken for numerous disputes about foreclosures on home loans following the problems stemming from sub-prime mortgages.
2. In Guyana, a Russian-owned bauxite company is using mediation to try to resolve disputes with the union about wages and the sacking of workers.
3. In the Middle East, the Côte d'Ivoire, Bosnia and elsewhere, mediators have been called in to work at a national level with warring parties.
4. The Vatican acted as mediator in the Beagle Channel dispute between Argentina and Chile over the ownership of the PNL island group.
5. Mediation has been used in New Zealand in connection with a rift between a Commonwealth Games medallist and her coach.
6. In Australia, the defamation action brought against the Premier of Queensland, Anna Bligh, by Clive Palmer in 2009 was resolved through mediation.

Summary

- Mediation is an essential part of a lawyer's toolkit.
- Its primary place in the dispute resolution spectrum is between negotiation and more formal proceedings.
- Your fee income can increase and your client base can grow when mediation is used appropriately.
- If you fail to discuss mediation with clients, your competitors undoubtedly will.
- The standards developed by your professional body may require you to consider all options for your clients.
- Access to justice is a cornerstone of our society.
- Many other countries have already seen the benefits of mediation.

Notes

1. Rushton, M., 'Effective mediation advocacy', *The Mediator Magazine*, p. 6.
2. Mr Hanger became a QC in 1984 and is a highly regarded mediator, both in Australia and internationally. For a more comprehensive profile, see <www.iamed.org>
3. Menon, *Shaping the Future*, para. 25.
4. Agapiou and Clark, *An Investigation of Construction Lawyer Attitudes*.
5. Federation of the Swiss Watch Industry FH.
6. Law Society of Scotland, Guidance related to Rule B1.9.
7. Solicitors Regulation Authority, *Code of Conduct*.
8. Federation of Law Societies of Canada, *Model Code of Professional Conduct*.
9. Lord Chancellor's Department, *Access to Justice*, Chapter 1, para. 7(d).
10. Court of Session, *Report of the Scottish Civil Courts Review*: 169.
11. Malcolm and O'Donnell, *A Guide to Mediating in Scotland*: vii.
12. Directive 2008/52/EC.
13. Directive 2008/52/EC: (3).
14. Directive 2013/11/EU: (4).
15. S. 8 (2) (b).
16. Directive 2008/52/EC, Article 6.1.
17. Brussels, 19.04.2002, COM (2002) 196 final, Green Paper.
18. COM (2002) 196 final, 3.2.2.3 and Question 18.
19. Menon, *Shaping the Future*, para. 50.
20. Court of Session, *Report of the Scottish Civil Courts Review*: 311.
21. Attree, *Alternative Dispute Resolution*.

Chapter 2

KEY PRINCIPLES

When deciding which form of dispute resolution to recommend to a client, it is helpful to understand the key principles of mediation. As you see from the diagrams in Chapter 1, some of these differ from the alternative forms of dispute resolution. There is no definitive number of principles, and commentators often differ on the sanctity of some of them. The five principles which follow are those which I find are key in discussions with potential users of mediation and their advisers:

1. Voluntary
   a. The parties come to mediation of their own free will.
   b. A party can withdraw from mediation at any time.
   c. It is up to the parties whether or not they reach an agreement.
   d. The terms of any such agreement are only those which the parties want, so they maintain control over the outcome.
2. Confidential
   a. All discussions between the mediator and the parties are confidential, including those held pre-mediation.
   b. During private discussions between the mediator and a party, the mediator confirms what points, if any, may be passed to the other party. Nothing is conveyed to the other party without express permission.
3. Impartial and neutral
   a. The mediator remains neutral so does not take sides.
   b. The mediator does not express opinions, or give advice.
   c. The role of the mediator is to act as a facilitator to help the discussion between the parties.
   d. The mediator does not impose a decision on the parties.
4. Interest-focused
   a. Mediation aims to help the parties find their underlying concerns, rather than their stated positions.

5. Mutual gain
   a. The ideal outcome of mediation is one where each party's interests are satisfied (and possibly enhanced).
   b. The basis for the settlement does not have to be the same for each party.

Let me expand.

Voluntary

It is true that parties can leave mediation at any time and that it is up to them to decide the terms of any agreement reached. The point about coming to mediation 'willingly' raises some interesting issues for you to consider with your client.

In the UK, courts generally do not have the power to insist on mediation.[1] However, when awarding costs in England:

> The court must also have regard to –
> (a) the conduct of all the parties, including in particular –
>   (i) conduct before, as well as during, the proceedings; and
>   (ii) the efforts made, if any, before and during the proceedings in order to try to resolve the dispute . . .[2]

The practical impact of this can be seen in the case of *Halsey*. Mrs Halsey had brought an action against the Milton Keynes General NHS Trust alleging negligence surrounding the death of her husband. The inquest was inconclusive, but the claimant sought damages and offered to mediate with the Trust. It refused, on the basis that it did not admit any liability. When the matter came to court, Mrs Halsey was unsuccessful in her action but sought costs on the basis that the Trust had unreasonably refused to participate in mediation. The decision by the trial judge not to award costs was upheld on appeal, but in its judgment the Court laid down two key principles.

The first was that while the court has a duty to *encourage* the use of ADR, any attempt to make it compulsory would be in violation of Article 6[3] of the European Convention on Human Rights.[4] The second principle established that, if parties have refused to consider ADR, the court may award costs against them. However, this came with the proviso that it is up to the losing party to show that the refusal to mediate by the winner was unreasonable.

As Lord Justice Dyson said when delivering the judgment of the Court:

> All members of the legal profession who conduct litigation should now routinely consider with their clients whether their disputes are suitable for ADR. But we reiterate that the court's role is to encourage, not to compel.[5]

He goes on to say:

> A party who refuses even to consider whether a case is suitable for ADR is always at risk of an adverse finding at the costs stage of litigation, and particularly so where the court has made an order requiring the parties to consider ADR.[6]

This was taken further in *Earl of Malmesbury* v *Strutt & Parker*. In this case, the parties waived their rights to the confidentiality of mediation, so their discussions were put before the Court. In the opinion of Mr Justice Jack:

> a party who agrees to mediation but then causes the mediation to fail by his reason of unreasonable position in the mediation is in reality in the same position as a party who unreasonably refuses to mediate. In my view it is something which the court can and should take account of in the costs order in accordance with the principles considered in Halsey.[7]

While *Halsey* had focused on costs awarded to a successful party who had refused to mediate, Master O'Hare in *Reid* v *Buckinghamshire Healthcare NHS Trust* applied the principles to the losing party. He showed his disapproval by awarding indemnity costs against the defendant, who failed to respond for six weeks to an offer to mediate and then provided no acceptable reason for the unwillingness to participate.

Similarly, in *Bristow* v *The Princess Alexandra Hospital NHS Trust*,[8] Master Simons addressed the issue of the defendant's unreasonable refusal to mediate. While he had awarded various costs with an interest rate of 8 per cent, Master Simons regarded an increased rate as an inappropriate sanction for refusal to mediate, as this would benefit only the solicitors. He went on to say: 'However, there is a point of principle involved and in my judgment there should be a sanction.'[9] He awarded costs on an indemnity basis.

Similar disapproval was shown by the Court in Hong Kong in *Wu Yim Kwong Kingwind* v *Manhood Development Limited*. The successful Defendant had been awarded 80 per cent costs. However, the company's unreasonable refusal to mediate meant that the costs order *nisi* was subsequently varied so no costs were awarded.

In mediations where parties attend willingly, they are highly likely to resolve their dispute. For example, at the Edinburgh Sheriff Court Mediation Service, 79 per cent of cases which went to mediation over a three year period resulted in a written agreement between the parties, so that no further court action was required.[10] This is in line with 2009 statistics from The Netherlands Mediation Institute, where 86 per cent of mediations that year resulted in either full or partial agreement.[11] The Australian Mediation Association reports that over 85 per cent of mediations end in agreement between the parties.[12]

However, some legislation in Ireland goes against the principle of voluntary mediation in personal injury claims. Section 15 of the Civil Liability and Courts Act 2004 confers a power on the High Court to compel parties to mediate their differences. Mr Justice Kelly discusses this section in the Court's judgment in *Ryan* v *Walls Construction Ltd* contrasting the position in the Commercial Court. In O. 63A, r. 6(1)(xiii) of the Rules of the Superior Courts and the subsequent Mediation Conciliation Regulations of 2010, O. 56(A), judges are given the power to adjourn proceedings to allow parties to consider whether ADR may be suitable.

The Court in *Ryan* took the view that, when exercising the powers granted by section 15,

> the court should consider whether in the case of a definitive and reasoned refusal to consider settlement of an action the making of an order under section 15 would have any realistic prospect of assisting in reaching a settlement.[13]

Mr Justice Kelly went on to say: 'A court is entitled to bear in mind the poorer chance of success in a mediation which is not undertaken on a voluntary basis.' While acknowledging the prerogative of the legislature to enact S15, Mr Justice Kelly appears to consider compulsory mediation to be impractical.

From your client's point of view, there is no guarantee that her dispute will be resolved through mediation. However, you could justifiably tell her that if both parties come to the table willingly and with the desire to sort out the dispute, the chances of an agreement being reached are high. In the commercial, court and workplace mediations which I have undertaken, just over 80 per cent have settled.

Confidential

It may be essential, or reassuring, for your client to know that discussions at mediation are intended to be confidential. This is often a critical point in commercial mediations where a party may not want to run the risk of proprietary information entering the public domain during court proceedings. If your client or her business is high-profile, she may also wish to avoid any adverse publicity resulting from litigation.

The Agreement to Mediate which all participants sign at the start of the meeting covers the aspect of confidentiality. At Mediation Scotland our agreement includes the following:

Confidentiality

10. The entire process of the mediation, including all communications prior to the mediation and all related documents, is and will be kept private and confidential.

11. The Mediator will not disclose to any Party or Adviser any information provided by another Party or Adviser in confidence without the express consent of the Party or unless required by law or public policy.

12. The mediation shall be treated as privileged and will be conducted without prejudice to any action in the courts. This paragraph shall not apply where:
    i) The Parties agree to specific disclosure;
    ii) Disclosure is necessary to implement and enforce the Settlement Agreement;
    iii) The Parties are, or any other person is, required by law to make disclosure;
    iv) A Party discloses anything that is unlawful.

13. The Mediator may not act for either Party individually in any capacity with regard to the subject matter of the mediation.

14. No Party, Representative or Adviser may have access to the Mediator's notes or call the Mediator as witness in any proceedings related to any of the issues between them. Unless directed by the Court, the Mediator's opinion will be inadmissible in any subsequent proceedings which may take place between the Parties, Representatives or Advisers concerning the subject matter of the mediation.[14]

Confidentiality is a key benefit for workplace mediations as well. While the results of a formal grievance procedure are usually recorded on an employee's file, agreements reached at mediation are not. The warring members of staff may have dug themselves into entrenched positions such that it has become difficult for them to apologise or change their attitudes without a third-party intervention. The principle of confidentiality allows the parties to discuss openly what's gone wrong in the working relationship and decide how they want to improve the situation.

The breakdown may have occurred between a manager and an employee. The confidentiality of mediation is often welcomed by the manager, who may have realised that she hasn't handled a matter well, but doesn't want to lose face with other members of staff. At mediation there are no other employees there to take sides or pass judgement.

Your client may express concern about revealing information in case the other party tries to use it later if mediation proves unsuccessful. There are two ways you can discuss this with her.

The first is to suggest that she chooses what she wants to discuss at mediation and what she does not. This comes with the proviso that if the parties truly want to resolve the dispute, it is important that each is open and honest during the discussions. If your client says that she does not want to reveal particular information which you feel is critical to the mediation, then it is up to you to advise her of the potential impact of this choice.

The second point for reassurance relates to the role of the mediator. Part of the mediation process (which we will look at in more detail in Chapter 3) usually involves private discussions between your client and the mediator. The confidentiality of mediation extends to these discussions. In practical terms this means that anything discussed remains confidential, unless your client authorises the mediator to pass information to the other party. Towards the end of a private session, I always check with the party 'So you'd like me to tell them that you might be prepared to consider reducing your claim but only if they re-do the work?', or 'Is there anything of what you've told me that you don't want the other side to know?', or 'You've said you'd be willing to pay £10,000 compensation. Do you want me to tell them that at this stage?'.

In spite of your reassurances, your client may still be concerned that there is no guarantee that the other party won't breach confidentiality. My suggestion in these circumstances would be to explore a little further to find out why your client is so mistrusting of the other party. If it becomes obvious that one or both may come to mediation in bad faith, there may be little point in mediating. The likelihood of the parties reaching agreement is reduced, so you may consider that in this instance mediation is not an appropriate option for your client.

Practical example

Client   You say that mediation is confidential, but how do I know that Fred [the other party] won't tell other people what I've said?

You   At the start of the meeting, everyone signs an agreement, a contract, about the mediation process. Part of this is about the confidentiality of the discussions and outcomes. It would be very serious if Fred breached this agreement.

Client   But there's no guarantee that he won't, is there?

You   You're right. There's no absolute guarantee, but in my experience of mediation it is very unusual for the confidentiality to be broken. (Or: I've spoken to the mediator about this point and she tells me that it's very unusual for confidentiality to be broken.) Is there any particular reason why you think Fred may breach confidentiality?

Client   No, but I don't trust him an inch.

You   Fair enough. That's your view of him. Fred has said he's willing to mediate so it may be in this instance that he is prepared to be trustworthy. This is something for you to weigh up in your own mind when deciding whether to mediate or not. You did say that you want to try to sort out this dispute as quickly as possible, and mediation can help with that. I guess you need to balance the need to resolve matters with your concerns about confidentiality. It's up to you to decide which is more important to you, as, remember, mediation is voluntary.

At the start of this section, I write that discussions at mediation are *intended* to be confidential. You may wonder why I have added the emphasis.

As we saw earlier, parties can jointly waive their right to confidentiality.[15] The impact in this case was that the judge was able to consider the attitude of the parties during mediation. Without the waiver, the discussions would have remained confidential.

(However, a court may require a mediator to disclose information in the interests of justice. If you are interested in reading more about this, see Appendix 13, where I look at the case of Farm Assist.)

If your client is considering mediation in a family law matter in Scotland, the provisions of the Civil Evidence (Family Mediation) (Scotland) Act 1995 come into play (arguably only if the mediation is court-ordered). While the provisions of this Act purport to make the content of family mediations confidential, Clause 2 (1) (a) states:

> Nothing in section 1 of this Act shall prevent the admissibility as evidence in civil proceedings –
> . . . of information as to any contract entered into during family mediation or of the fact that no contract was entered into during such mediation . . .

In *FJM* v *GCM* there was argument that the written summary of the points agreed at mediation formed a 'contract' and was thus admissible in evidence. While The Honourable Lord Stewart did not have to rule on this particular point, he does say that 'Arguably the exception does apply'.[16]

I am not experienced in mediation of family matters, so I cannot provide a practical insight into the comments by His Lordship. As I don't want to lead practitioners astray by wrongly interpreting the legal meaning of 'contract', all I seek to do here is to highlight the point for you to investigate further before advising your client.

Impartial and neutral

One of the cornerstones of this process is the impartiality of the mediator. Of course, this neutral stance is not unique. Arbitrators are usually appointed jointly by the parties so they too are impartial adjudicators. Judges are allocated by the court. In the UK it is not possible for one party to select a judge who she thinks will be favourably disposed towards her point of view.

So why is the neutrality worth mentioning? In my view it links with the overall style of mediation. There are a number of different styles, which are discussed in Appendix 17. In your work, it is likely that the most common style you will encounter is 'facilitative'. For your client, this means that the mediator acts as a facilitator of the discussions between the parties, and that she does not take sides or give advice. This neutrality of the mediator provides reassurance to the parties and encourages open and frank discussion. Neither party has to 'prove' anything to the mediator so she can decide who's right and who's wrong. Compare this with arbitrators, judges and juries who look at the evidence presented and make decisions on the basis of whether they believe it or not.

A mediator is not there to make binding decisions. This provides added reassurance for your client in private sessions. She is likely to feel more comfortable about talking openly with the mediator and discussing where, in hindsight, she may have made a mistake in her dealings with the other party.

In my experience, the very fact that I have no vested interest in the agreements which the parties may reach assists my standing as a neutral. I can play a devil's advocate role without your client feeling that I am taking the side of the other party. She recognises that I am there to help her thought processes and not to defend the position of the other side.

Rant

One of the reasons I am not a supporter of in-house mediators for workplace disputes is that this neutrality may not be a reality. How can someone who is likely to know the parties, or at the very least be liable to encounter them again after the mediation, be seen to be neutral? In spite of reassurances which may be given, parties often still believe that management is going to be told what was discussed, or that their career prospects may be hampered if they say too much during mediation.

Interest-focused

Disputing parties often have entrenched positions. Another characteristic of mediation is that it helps the parties reconsider their stance and look at what lies beneath – the interest. What this means for your client is that mediation can help resolve what she *really* wants to achieve, rather than limiting discussions to simply what is 'said'. It's a bit like an iceberg. The part you can see above the surface is the stated position of the party ('You did a lousy job installing my kitchen and I want my money back'). Initially hidden from sight are the underlying needs and interests which support this position ('I want the cupboard doors to hang properly' – need; 'I really enjoy cooking so I want to be happy when I'm in the kitchen' – interest). Mediation helps lower the level of the waves to reveal the interests.

As an example, your client wants to bring a civil action against a neighbour who has built a fence which prevents access to a right of way. The neighbour is refusing to remove the offending structure because she says that access is still available through adjacent common land. If your client chooses the litigation route, everyone will focus on the legal rights and wrongs, title deeds will be scrutinised, and a judgment made. One party will win and one party will lose.

By contrast, mediation helps the parties peel back the layers to understand why your client is demanding access and why the neighbour wants to keep the fence. During discussions, they slowly reveal their real interests. Your client wants to be able to get her rubbish bin out easily for collection. It is difficult for her to manoeuvre the bin across the rough ground of the common land. The neighbour wants the fence to keep her child safe. (This example is loosely based on an actual mediation where the action had reached the Court of Session. Once the interests were in the open and discussed, the parties reached an agreement which suited them both.) So the dispute wasn't about rights of way as such; it was about the impact of the fence on daily life. One person wanted an easier bin day; the other wanted to protect her child.

Sidebar

In this book I often refer to 'litigation' or 'court action' as an alternative to mediation. Of course, the vast majority of disputes do not end up in court. What I seek to compare is the *adversarial* nature of the litigation route, with the *let's work it out together* focus of mediation. Even if matters are settled on the steps of the court, the longevity of the dispute has often exacerbated the feelings of distrust, hurt or anger between the parties. If there is a power imbalance between them, the 'weaker' may agree reluctantly to a solution because she feels there is no other option

At mediation, these issues can be addressed and the parties are more likely to leave feeling that the best possible solution for each has been reached.

Another oft-quoted example is that of the two children and the orange. The children are arguing. Each says he 'needs' the piece of fruit. Along comes the judge (Exasperated Parent: 'EP'), cuts the orange in half and distributes the spoils. The kids are still grumbling. EP replies: 'But you both said you needed the orange. Now you've got half each, so that's fair.' The Very Clever Parent (VCP) first of all asks the kids why they need the orange. Little Johnny says he wants the peel for zest for the biscuits he's cooking (aha! – the interest is that he wants to cook). Little Freddy wants to eat the 'squelchy inside bits' (interest – the poor child is starving). Now that VCP knows the interests of each, a better solution is reached and peace reigns.

What, by the way, was the solution to the fence dispute? They agreed that the back of the fence would be moved in a couple of feet to provide a wider path across the common land. The younger neighbour's suggestion that she take the rubbish bin out each week was discussed but rejected. Instead she agreed to put paving stones down as a path so the bin could be wheeled without difficulty. There was even resolution about how wide the path needed to be so the bin could be taken round a corner without problems.

Mutual gain

The most satisfying outcome of mediation is where the parties' interests have not only been met but enhanced. The reason this is important for your client is that a dispute which otherwise might result in a hollow victory for her can result in an unexpected benefit. Have a look at the case study about Mr Jones and the Car Company. Picture yourself as the Company's solicitor and consider what you might have said when the business told you they were being taken to court. Then think about the actual outcome of the mediation. How satisfied would your client have been if they had defended the court action (possibly successfully) compared to how satisfied they were with the outcome of the mediation?

Case study

Mr Jones bought a car at auction for his son. After a month the turbo failed and had to be replaced. Some time later the engine seized up without warning and the car became worthless. Investigations by Mr Jones revealed that the manufacturer (Car Company) was aware of the problems with this engine type and had introduced an extended five-year policy to cover failures. However, no support was available for cars bought outside the Car Company network or without a full service history. Mr Jones alleged a cover-up by the Car Company, saying that it had misled the public by not providing full information. His argument was that a potential purchaser would have no way of knowing they were buying goods unsuitable for purpose. Mr Jones brought a court action seeking £3,150 plus interest and expenses as compensation for the misrepresentation by the Car Company. At mediation the Car Company representatives said they had no obligation to Mr Jones as he had not purchased the car from them. Mr Jones readily admitted this, but the subtext was that he wanted to give the Car Company a hard time and get some money out of them. He was prepared to follow through with court action if necessary.

During the mediation Mr Jones revealed that he had bought cars from the Car Company over the years because he considered them reliable. The Car Company appeared keen to avoid the publicity associated with court actions, although this was not specifically mentioned. The parties reached a Settlement Agreement whereby Mr Jones dropped the legal proceedings and the Car Company sold him a new car with a substantial discount. Both were winners in this outcome. The Car Company retained a customer; Mr Jones gained a car.

Another aspect of the 'mutual gain' characteristic is that the *basis* for agreement need not be the same for each party. For example, Mr Jones may have accepted the terms because he had caused the Car Company some grief through the hassle of attending court and then the mediation. As an added bonus, he's happy to buy another car knowing he's been given a substantial discount. The Car Company has accepted the same terms, because it has retained a loyal customer, avoided adverse publicity, sold another car and still made a profit.

Summary

- Five important principles of mediation – voluntary, confidential, impartial/neutral, interest-focused and mutual gain.
- The litigation route is adversarial; the mediation option encourages resolution which satisfies both parties.
- Your client does not have to agree anything at mediation that she doesn't want to.
- The discussions remain private in most circumstances.
- The mediator is not there to attack your client, or to cast aspersions on her beliefs.
- Mediation is sometimes like an artichoke. You peel back all the outer matter until you get to the heart of the matter.
- The outcome of a satisfactory mediation is that each party feels that progress in some form has been made.

Notes

1. Pre-application Protocol and Practice Direction which supplement the Family Proceedings Rules came into effect in April 2011. Couples in England and Wales who are planning to contest their separation terms must consider mediation before litigation.
2. The Civil Procedure Rules 1998, No.3132 (L17) part 44.4 (3) (a).
3. '. . . everyone is entitled to a fair and public hearing within a reasonable time by an independent and impartial tribunal established by law.'
4. Convention for the Protection of Human Rights and Fundamental Freedoms CETS No. 005.
5. *Halsey* para. 11.
6. *Halsey* para. 33.
7. *Earl of Malmesbury* para. 72.
8. See also *Garritt-Critchley and Others* v *Ronnan and Another [2014] EWHC 1774 (Ch)* where indemnity costs were awarded following an unreasonable refusal to mediate. See also *PGF II SA v OMFS Company 1 Ltd [2013] EWCA Civ 1288.*
9. *Bristow* para. 10.
10. Collation of figures from reports of Edinburgh Sheriff Court Mediation Service from September 2004 to August 2007, written by the author.
11. Gathier, *The Situation Regarding Mediation.*
12. <http://ama.asn.au/what-is-mediation/> (last accessed 1 May 2016).
13. *Ryan,* para. 59.
14. Mediation Scotland, Agreement to Mediate: see Appendix 5.
15. *Earl of Malmesbury.*
16. *FJM* para. 21.

Chapter 3

MEDIATION IN PRACTICE

When to consider mediation

Mediation can be used at any stage in a dispute, not just at the beginning. Even if a court date has already been set, you can consider mediation. It can be used to narrow issues before or during litigation. In ongoing business relationships, mediation can also be used to resolve differences before they escalate. Mediation may be appropriate when or after an employment grievance has been raised. Ideally, mediation should be considered as soon as potential conflict is identified.

However – and in my view, this is a big 'however' – parties are more open to the idea of mediation if they have reached a stage where they want to 'sort this thing out'. The reason I add this rider is that we humans often need to do something physical before we start to consider rational options. We argue, get into fisticuffs, cry, shout, undermine or try other tactics to conquer the opposition. Some people thrive on this stage. Others never want to move from it, as the dispute has become the focus of their lives. What would they do with themselves if they didn't have this conflict to worry about? (I have seen this frequently in Sheriff Court mediations. One party is reluctant to resolve matters at mediation because for the past X years the dispute has provided an interest for him. He's not quite sure what he'd do tomorrow morning if this matter were at an end.)

You may then wonder how you know what stage your client is at. Unfortunately, there's no clear answer to this – unless he says 'I want to sort this thing out now'. The knowledge comes from your experience of dealing with that client and with others in conflict. My suggestion is to go with your instincts, and after some successes and failures you will start to recognise when the client is likely to be open to resolution options.

Sidebar

While awareness of mediation is growing in the UK, there remain many potential users who do not know how it works. They are likely to have seen courtroom dramas on TV, but probably not mediation. Party litigants often talk of 'having my day in court' as though the world will sit up and take notice and after an hour everything will be sorted in their favour. When it comes to mediation, they do not have a picture of how things will play out. Later, we'll look at different ways of explaining the mediation process to your clients.

Your client's objectives

The first thing to consider is what your client wants out of possible mediation. Does he want to recover money, sort out division of property, or hang the other party out to dry?

I cannot begin to remember the number of times in my past 40 years in business when I've been told that a dispute is all about a 'point of principle'. If we all really had such strong principles the world would be a great place. Only rarely have I mediated a dispute which truly was about principles.

Case study

A middle-aged couple had a driveway laid. In their view the work was sub-standard, but their efforts to persuade the builder to rectify his work proved futile. The contractor's perspective was that the job was fine and that 'these people' were too fussy. The couple brought a court action claiming reimbursement of the monies already paid for the work. Both parties agreed to participate in mediation.

During mediation the couple said that their priority was not to get the money back. They wanted the contractor to know that he couldn't get away with doing shoddy work; they had brought the action because it was a 'point of principle'. (Mediator's eyes roll back in head.)

As part of the mediation process, the contractor was asked to listen to the couple as they explained how distressing they had found the whole experience of the problems with the driveway. Slowly, he started to realise the impact of his earlier attitude towards their complaints.

As the problems with the driveway had already been fixed by another builder, there was no opportunity for him to re-do the work. While offering his apologies, he was visibly concerned at the prospect of having to repay monies to the couple as he was a small one-man business.

> During discussions facilitated by the mediator, a solution was agreed
> and put in writing. The builder apologised to the couple, acknowledged
> that poor workmanship caused upset and distress, and agreed that he
> would be aware of that in dealings with other customers. As part of the
> settlement, he agreed to pay £100 to a charity chosen by the couple.
> Principles upheld and lessons learned.

Let's look at a simple example of consideration of the mediation option. Your client bought a motorcycle for £10,000. It's been an absolute lemon and has had a series of small problems. While the garage who sold it to him has fixed each problem, it's been a huge inconvenience for him having to take it for repairs. He's come to you because he feels that there must have been a breach of contract if the garage has sold him a bike which is not perfect. He says he wants his money back. The garage is denying any liability because in their view the bike is fine now.

One option – start proceedings against the garage alleging breach of contract under the relevant Sale of Goods legislation. You explain the costs of this to your client, the length of time involved and the likelihood of success.

Another option – find out what his real objective is. Is it his £10,000 back or is it a reliable motorcycle? If he says the money, then what guarantee does he have that problems won't recur when he buys a replacement? How much will he have left from the £10,000 once he's paid the legal costs? You find out that he's always bought this brand of motorbike and this is the first time he's had problems. He wants a bike that doesn't have annoying little problems. Then he tells you he likes this brand as he feels it's good for his image. Aha! – so is image more important than the money? Mediation may be an appropriate option here.

Possible outcome – Your client agrees to pay the garage £1,000 and they replace his bike with the latest model. The garage benefits from selling the old bike to someone else, retaining a customer and avoiding potential negative publicity from your client telling all his mates. Your client is happy because he now has the latest model, which will be good for his image. On top of that he has a reliable bike. For both of them, trust is restored.

The other party's objectives

You may feel that to suggest mediation to the other side shows a sign of weakness. In Chapter 4 we look at how to 'sell' mediation from a position of strength. In the interim, let's look at the other party's possible objectives.

Case study

A dispute has arisen between two global companies – one based in Germany and another in Italy. The German company, Great Big Coal Miners ('Miners'), wants to take legal action against your Italian client, Enormous Equipment Suppliers ('Suppliers'), claiming damages for failure to provide equipment to the required standard and for the consequent loss of production.

Miners paid Suppliers €2.5 million for a large piece of equipment – a dragline – to use in its open-cut coalmining operations. The dragline keeps breaking down, which means that mining has to stop until repairs are carried out. This causes Miners a financial loss of about €50,000 an hour.

Suppliers says that Miners used the wrong type of lubricant on the bearings during the first routine maintenance. This has caused the ongoing problems.

Miners are not entirely sure what lubricant was used by the maintenance team as the records were accidentally shredded.

Your client, Suppliers, is facing the prospect of protracted legal proceedings – an idea which the CEO Silvio Bruschetta does not relish. Mr Bruschetta believes that Miners is to blame for the problems, but he does not want to lose this major client, or face the risk of Miners telling others that there have been problems with equipment supplied by them.

From the other party's point of view, is mediation worth considering? You assess the situation and realise that it's highly likely Miners will be concerned about the amount of money it is losing when the dragline is not working. So, a point in favour of them considering mediation is that it is usually much more speedily than formal litigation. A meeting can be arranged in a matter of days if necessary.

What's your understanding of Miners' other concerns? How important is the ongoing business relationship to Miners? Can it readily source equipment of this scale? If Miners cuts one supplier out, would it restrict the company's negotiating power on price? What about the problem of the missing maintenance records? Would that cast doubt in the mind of the Court about liability? If litigation proved unsuccessful, what impact would that have on the company's share price?

> Given all these points, what might Miners' objectives be? You surmise that they want to ensure their share price is not affected by this dispute. If that's their objective, then you would focus on the confidentiality aspect of mediation when you are 'selling' mediation to Miners' lawyers.
>
> And so on . . .

Don't be discouraged by the seemingly impossible stated objectives of your client. He's likely to have an initial standpoint which he clings to steadfastly.

Case study

Home-owner	You did a lousy job installing my windows so *I'm not going to pay your bill*.
Window installer	I told you at the beginning that the price didn't include the painting of the frames. The windows fit perfectly. *You have to pay me*.

After discussions, an effective mediator helps the parties to recognise their real objectives and interests. Perhaps the home-owner wants to ensure he pays only when the work is completed properly. He is very proud of his house and he wants his neighbours to think highly of him because he can afford new windows. The window installer needs to be paid because his overdraft is spiralling out of control. He's fed up with people arguing about the price of his work and he wishes customers would realise that he's good at what he does. The meeting may evolve to:

1. an acknowledgement that in reality one window doesn't fit as well as it should but the others are perfect
2. there was a misunderstanding about the painting (the installer had referred to painting only the primer on the windows; the home-owner took that to mean a finished paint job)
3. an acknowledgement that the windows have improved the appearance of the property and have been a godsend this winter.

A possible outcome may be:

1. home-owner pays 80 per cent of the bill now and installer fixes the ill-fitting window once that money is received
2. home-owner pays for the paint, installer reduces his labour costs by 5 per cent and paints the windows (cost of this work to be limited to £1,000)
3. remaining costs to be paid by home-owner on final day of painting by cash or bank cheque
4. all to be finished by 28 February.

What situations are suitable?

In essence, mediation can be used in most situations. Andrew Floyer Acland refers to mediation as the 'adjustable spanner in the toolkit'.[1] It doesn't matter how big or small the dispute is, whether it involves just two people or many, whether it's between a David and a Goliath, or whether the parties will ever see each other again. The most important point is that the parties must be *willing* to mediate to have a reasonable chance of resolving the dispute.

Here are some areas where mediation is used, and a few brief examples:

1. Commercial
   a. Alleged breach of contract for failure to provide goods to the agreed standard. Differing interpretations of the standard.
   b. Failure to maintain commercial premises during the term of the lease resulting in loss of value of the property at time of sale.
   c. Protection of designs owned by a UK company, where the products were supplied in another country. Allegedly, one supplier was copying a design and selling the goods locally at low prices.
2. Executories, wills and trusts
   a. A dispute over the management of a large estate held in trust was resolved by the managers agreeing to resign and appoint a third party in their stead.
   b. Family members disagreeing about disposal of assets referred to in a home-made will.
3. Family
   a. A situation where a couple want to separate but for financial reasons must stay together in the family home.
   b. Child custody and access.
   c. Division of assets.
   d. Encouraging a child to return home (for example, Amber mediation, which is a joint initiative of Edinburgh Cyrenians and SACRO).
4. Workplace
   a. Colleagues in a small office who had not spoken to each other for three years after an allegedly offensive comment was made at a staff Christmas party.

    b. Grievance held by a member of staff against a manager which had been dealt with internally. Mediation was used to help them agree how to work together in the future.

5. Creative industries

    a. In the USA, mediation has been used in this sector for a number of years. Research[2] carried out in 1999 showed an increase in the use of mediation in an industry which often needs creative solutions to disputes. The majority of attorneys who participated in the survey preferred mediation to litigation because of the efficiency of the process, the probability that working relationships could be maintained, and the fact that settlement agreements could be tailor-made.

    b. As Danielle Cara Newman points out in another article,[3] 'These disputes typically center on time-sensitive, costly and confidential issues'. (Though I would suggest that this is often the situation for most commercial disputes.) Newman goes on to show how litigation[4] pending at the time between Lady Gaga and her personal assistant could have been dealt with more satisfactorily through mediation than through litigation.

6. Medical

    a. Mediation has been used when children brought a claim following the death of their mother during surgery.

    b. The NHS Litigation Authority in England has produced a practical guide for users of mediation of clinical negligence claims.[5] Table 1 of the guide compares how various forms of dispute resolution do or don't meet the needs of parties.

    c. Mediation is an ideal way for families to resolve conflict in situations where an elderly relative is unable to make decisions, often owing to dementia.

7. Personal injury

    a. A compensation claim was brought against the Ministry of Defence (MOD) by the parents of a soldier who accidentally shot himself during a training exercise. The use of mediation gave the father the opportunity to tell the MOD directly how his son's death had affected his family. It also allowed the MOD to express its sorrow to the parents and to avoid any argument at a trial about contributory negligence.

8. Complaints

   a. In Scotland, complaints about legal practitioners are channelled through the Scottish Legal Complaints Commission. Where the complaint is about a breach of the Law Society's service standards, the parties may be offered the opportunity to mediate. These meetings are time-limited to three hours (though the average is around 1.5 hours). Resolutions have included a complainer accepting an explanation about delays in dealing with a matter, an apology by the practitioner, financial compensation, and an offer to do work for no fee.

   b. In England and Wales, the Legal Ombudsman is responsible for dealing with complaints about legal service providers, claims management companies and accountants (in probate matters). While there is no specific path of mediation, the rules encourage early resolution:

> The Legal Ombudsman will try to resolve complaints at the earliest possible stage, by whatever means it considers appropriate – including formal resolution.[6]

In the Business Plan there is specific reference to mediation:

> The key objective during this stage of the process [resolution] will be to facilitate informal settlement between the two parties wherever possible. In some cases, this may require making use of mediation techniques.[7]

   c. Since July 2014 the NHS Litigation Authority in England has offered mediation for complaints 'in all suitable cases involving a fatality or elderly care',[8] and it provides an informative users' guide.[9]

   d. Legislation[10] is in place for the use of 'conciliation or mediation for complaints about the NHS in Scotland', but to date I cannot find information which shows that the organisation has embraced the use of mediation wholeheartedly.

9. Shipping

   a. While arbitration is the most common form of dispute resolution for the maritime sector, mediation was used in Greece in 2010. A Scottish mediator who is also a member of EMMA (Eastern Mediterranean Mediators Association) worked with parties to the dispute, the details of which obviously remain confidential. (Shipping disputes typically include matters such as bills of lading, charter-party agreements and unauthorised diversions.)

10. Community

   a. The use of mediation in community disputes is invaluable, as it allows for voices to be heard and local resolutions to be developed.

   b. Disputes may, for example, be about dogs barking, antisocial behaviour, children, harassment and noise.

   c. Community mediators need specialised skills. They work with the parties to help them develop long-term solutions if they must continue to live in close proximity to one another.

   d. It is rare for lawyers to be involved in such mediations.

11. Neighbour

   a. In the first edition of this book, I linked 'community' and 'neighbour' disputes together and suggested that the terms were interchangeable. However, following subsequent case law, I think it is now appropriate to separate them and interpret 'neighbour disputes' as ones where the parties have involved lawyers. This is not to say that mediation is always the answer, because as Jackson LJ acknowledges:

> Of course there are many cases where a strict determination of rights and liabilities is what the parties require. The courts stand ready to deliver such a service to litigants and must do so as expeditiously and economically as practicable.[11]

His Lordship goes on to say:

> But before embarking upon full blooded adversarial litigation parties should first explore the possibility of settlement. In neighbour disputes of the kind now before the court (and of which I have seen many similar examples) if negotiation fails, mediation is the obvious and constructive way forward.

   b. My favourite part of the judgment of Jackson LJ is when he refers to the considerable costs which were accrued before mediation was even mentioned:

> If the parties were driven by concern for the well-being of lawyers, they could have given half that sum to the Solicitors Benevolent Association and then resolved their dispute for a modest fraction of the monies left over.[12]

c. Similar sentiments were made by Elias LJ in a case about a right of way on farmland. His Lordship says:

> This is a case which was crying out for mediation, even assuming that it could not have been settled more informally than that. It ought never to have come near a court, and with a modicum of good will on both sides, it would not have done so.[13]

12. Landlord/tenant

a. Mediation is used frequently for issues over return of deposits which have been withheld owing to alleged damage to the property. It is especially helpful in situations where a young student has not realised that he may be personally liable for damage if his housemates disappear.

13. Peer

a. The use of peer mediation in both primary and secondary schools is increasingly widespread – especially in Northern Ireland and Scotland.

b. Trained student mediators (some as young as eight years old) facilitate discussions between classmates who have clashed.

14. Additional Support Needs

a. Under the Education (Additional Support for Learning) (Scotland) Act 2004 local authorities are required to offer mediation to help resolve issues with parents and/or children about additional support needs.

b. Section 15 of the Act reiterates the voluntary nature of mediation and also says that the parent or child should not have to pay for this service.

15. Planning

a. In early 2010 the Scottish Government launched a pilot study to assess the effectiveness of mediation in the planning process. Unfortunately, I cannot find any evaluation of this project to include in the second edition of this book. The Scottish Government website does include the publication *A Guide to the Use of Mediation in the Planning System in Scotland*.

b. In England, the 2010 report *Mediation in Planning* recognises that mediation is not always appropriate. However, the authors write that when it is 'we strongly recommend that the planning system now embraces mediation'.[14] The report contains many interesting case studies, including one which refers to the importance of the solicitor's presence.[15]

16. Construction
    a. While you are probably familiar with the use of arbitration for construction disputes, mediation may be appropriate as well.
    b. According to research[16] carried out in 2009, users of mediation for construction disputes reported significant cost savings. The authors also note that 'Even where the mediation did not result in a settlement it was not always viewed negatively'.[17] (The fuller work was completed in 2010 if you are interested in reading more about this area.)[18]
    c. Research undertaken into the attitude of Scottish construction lawyers towards the use of mediation shows high levels of satisfaction and a recognition that it is a useful tool to be able to offer to clients.[19]

17. Other areas
    a. Church
    b. Civil recovery (I have mediated in proceedings brought under the Proceeds of Crime Act.)
    c. Discrimination
    d. Environmental
    e. Franchising
    f. Mergers & Acquisitions
    g. Restorative justice

Sidebar

I'm often asked if mediation is suitable for complaints by a third party against lawyers. Examples of this might be when your client is:

- an insurance company but the complainer is the policy holder with whom you dealt on a day-to-day basis
- the purchaser of a property and the person complaining about you is the buyer
- the Executor and the third party is a beneficiary

The short answer to the question is 'It depends'. For fruitful discussions to take place at mediation, you need to be able to talk openly. This may not be possible, because of the duty of confidentiality you owe to your client. In such situations, mediation would be pointless.

However, in circumstances where discussions can take place without breaching confidentiality, mediation may be possible. In one situation, the purchaser complained about poor service provided by the seller's solicitor. The purchaser had arranged with the solicitor to collect the keys for the property on a Friday afternoon before a holiday weekend. When he arrived at the agreed time, the solicitor's office was closed and the purchaser was unable to contact anyone from the firm. This resulted in various practical difficulties and stress for the purchaser.

Mediation was able to take place because the matters of concern did not relate to the solicitor's client. At mediation, the solicitor apologised unreservedly and accepted responsibility for the mistake. He explained what steps had been put in place to prevent a similar occurrence in the future. The next day he personally delivered a cheque for the small amount of compensation as agreed, as well as a bottle of whisky. (Well, it was Scotland . . .)

Situations where mediation may not be suitable

Beneficial though mediation is, it is not always the most appropriate option for dispute resolution. For example, mediation may not be suitable if:

1. A point of law needs to be clarified or a precedent established. This was recognised by the Court in *Daniels* v *Metropolitan Police Commissioner*. Ms Daniels had brought a claim against her former employer after she had been injured by falling from a police horse. She was unsuccessful in her action, but argued that she should not bear the defendant's costs because it had refused to participate in mediation. The counter-argument was that the case had to come to court, otherwise there would be a 'flood of claims' from other police officers. The appeal court upheld the decision that costs should follow success and commented:

> It would be entirely reasonable for a defendant, especially a public body, to take the view that it would contest an unfounded claim in order to deter similarly unfounded claims. If defendants routinely faced unfounded claims and wanted to take a stand, the court should be slow to categorise such conduct as unreasonable and penalise them through the payment of costs if the litigation was successful.[20]

2. A party is not willing to participate. As discussed in Chapter 2, one of the key principles of mediation is that it is voluntary. In some jurisdictions, though, mediation is mandatory, but I can never see the point of this. The chances of parties coming to the table wanting to discuss issues openly and honestly with a view to sorting out a workable solution are much reduced. (My scepticism doesn't mean to say that mandatory mediation never works. In family law disputes, mandatory mediation often means that it is the first time the parties have really sat down and listened to each other. They can then work together to develop solutions regarding children and property.)

   Sometimes, though, the reluctance to mediate is based on misunderstandings of the process and what may be achieved. If you have a client who is unwilling to participate, dig a little deeper into his reasons. Is it that he feels he will be forced into an agreement he does not want? Does he think the other side will just use what they are told for later litigation?

   In my experience, once a potential party's concerns are clarified, he is usually willing to give mediation a try. However, and for me this is another big 'however', if I have the feeling that the person is still reluctant, I draw back. I advise him that I'm not going to twist his arm; it's his decision.

3. An injunction is required.
4. It is in the public interest that a matter comes before the court.
5. One party is a vexatious litigant. He or she is unlikely to come to mediation in the necessary spirit – that is, wanting to sort out a mutually acceptable solution.
6. There is a power imbalance between the parties to the extent that one party would be intimidated by the other.

Tip

Once a mediation meeting is under way, the mediator ensures that one party does not unfairly dominate proceedings to the detriment of others. However, before it gets to the stage of the actual mediation, you should consider whether the other party is likely to try to use his size or style to manipulate the process. Take for example a situation where your client is a tenant in a commercial retail development. The property owner Big Shop Ltd is a large international conglomeration which focuses solely on the bottom line and historically has used its size to bully tenants into arduous contractual terms. The company is trying to enforce terms relating to rent increases in spite of its failure to maintain the building in some areas. Your client wants to stay in the premises for the next three years, but before paying the increased rent he wants the company to replace the flooring outside his shop as its poor condition is deterring customers. In theory this could be an ideal dispute to be resolved through mediation.

However, your discussions to date with the company's representatives lead you to believe that Big Shop will maintain the line 'Pay the increase or we'll throw you out'.

They have initiated legal proceedings against your client.

In this instance you should weigh up the likelihood of the company coming to mediation in good faith with a willingness to try to resolve matters. If the indicators are that its representatives will attend with no real intention of reaching a solution acceptable to both sides, then your client may as well save the mediation costs. (Remember, though, that you need to balance this with the position of the Court on offers/rejection of mediation discussed in Chapter 2.)

In my experience, the bluff or timidity of parties in the lead-up to mediation isn't always reflected in the meeting itself. One of the roles of the mediator is to ensure that each party has the time and the space to put his point of view. However, if one party has already been using his physical, financial or market clout to try to intimidate the other, then mediation would be inappropriate in most circumstances.

Sidebar

Throughout this book, when I mention 'parties' I write as though there are only two. While this is the most usual situation, there can of course be any number of separate parties. For example, in a planning mediation, there may be property owners, developers, local residents and planning officials. The logistics are scaled up to deal with the additional people. If there are a large number of parties, it may be necessary to have two mediators. This is something to discuss when you are choosing a mediator.

When does mediation work best?

In my experience, the essential factor in predicting whether mediation will be helpful or not is the willingness of the parties. By this I mean their desire to participate in the process, to listen to each other and to be prepared to develop solutions which are acceptable to all. When I'm asked if mediation is appropriate for a particular situation, my first question is usually 'Do the parties want to try to sort things out?'. If one party is hesitant, it doesn't mean all is lost. An effective lawyer or mediator is able to explain the process, answer questions about the process and generally provide that party with enough information for him to make an informed choice about whether to participate.

Of course, thorough preparation by all, and the capabilities of the mediator, have a huge impact on the meeting. However, all this can be for nought if the parties don't truly commit, either before or during the mediation, to trying to find solutions. (For some people the dispute itself becomes the centre of their lives. Deep down they don't really want to resolve matters because they aren't sure what will then fill the gap in their existence. Sad but true, as can be seen in much litigation in the lower courts.)

Sidebar

A few years ago I had a mediation experience which still haunts me. The details of the dispute are not relevant here, but of particular interest was that the Pursers had brought their legal action using a lawyer (let's call him Fred) on a 'no win, no fee basis'. Fred was keen for his clients to try mediation and had been my point of contact in setting up the arrangements for the day. However, Fred had brought into the picture another firm (let's call them ABC), who are considered one of the best in their locality. At mediation there were three lawyers from ABC physically present, but their body language strongly suggested they did not want to be there.

From my experience, I thought that this dispute had a reasonable chance of being settled at mediation. However, the process was sabotaged by the lack of co-operation (and aggressiveness) on the part of the representatives of ABC, who made no attempt to help their clients work towards a solution. Needless to say, there was no agreement between the parties.

While the parties had been willing to mediate, one set of lawyers obviously wasn't. What a waste of everyone's time and money.

The flow of mediation

There is no set format for a mediation meeting. In general, though, the life cycle of mediation process rolls from considering the dispute resolution methods to choosing the mediator, preparing thoroughly,

ensuring the right people are at the table, developing options for settlement, and following up the outcome. The usual players involved
are the clients and the mediator, with other appropriate participants
(for example, lawyers, accountants, family members or friends).

'What about', you may well ask, 'persuading the disputing parties
to agree to participate in mediation?' Excellent question! More on
that in Chapter 4, but for now you may find it helpful to understand
what actually happens at the mediation itself.

Mediators may vary in how they approach a meeting, so I will
describe the path I generally follow in a straightforward situation
where there are only two people involved and no lawyers are present.
You may feel that some of the points are a bit pedantic, but there are
reasons for each, which I cover in more depth in Appendix 9.

The parties or their lawyers have provided me with background
information, so I've done my preparation. On the day there will be a
minimum of two rooms available.

The parties usually arrive separately, so I greet them, offer refreshments and make small talk. Once the preliminaries are out of the way,
I move the first party (let's call him Tim) into one of the rooms, point
out where he should sit and leave him to it. I wait outside the room
for Jack (the other person) to turn up – greet, cuppa, weather discussion, and then invite him into the room where Tim is waiting. (While
Jack's helping himself to coffee, I quickly pop in to tell Tim that Jack
has arrived.)

I guide Jack towards Tim, make the introductions and then direct
Jack to sit where I suggest. Once everyone is settled, I thank them
both for coming and cover any housekeeping. I then move quickly to
the Agreement to Mediate. Both Tim and Jack will have received a
draft copy of this from me in advance, with the invitation to contact
me if they have any questions. For the meeting I have prepared final
copies for us each to sign. I check if either has any questions, and if
not, I refer to the clause about confidentiality and remind them that
this is key to the discussions at mediation. We sign three copies and
retain one each.

I then explain my role in the process, remind the parties that mediation is voluntary, and tell them we have two rooms available so if either
wants a private discussion with me, we can use that. I will describe a
possible flow for the day. For example: 'As I mentioned to each of you
on the phone, I'd like to start by asking you to briefly tell the other
how you see the situation between you, and most importantly how

you would like to resolve your differences. While you're each having your say, I'd ask that the other person doesn't interrupt. So Tim, if Jack starts, I'd appreciate if you don't interrupt while he's speaking, and then vice versa for you, Jack, when it's Tim's turn. Do you both agree to that? Great, thanks for that. Once you've each had an opportunity to talk, then we can either stay together in this room or we can use both. We can play it by ear and see how things flow. Remember, do just say if you want a bit of breathing space or you want a private chat with me at any time. Does that sound all right? Great, who'd like to start?'

The time taken to get to this point is 5–10 minutes from when we're all seated.

Jack speaks, and I thank him but make no other comment. Tim speaks, ditto. I then thank them both for being so open and positive and summarise what each has said.

The rest of the meeting depends on the individuals. Sometimes they will start discussing matters directly with each other. It could be that they are still unsure where to begin, so I might help them establish priorities. We could all stay together or move to separate rooms straightaway. If they do separate, the parties will often come back together at different stages. Sometimes they may stay apart for the rest of the mediation. Of course this is not ideal, but it may be the best in a particular situation.

If the parties reach an agreement, I help them develop a form of words and write them down. I continue to reinforce the point that this is their agreement and that I am simply the scribe. For example:

Me	Jack, you said that you are willing to re-paint Tim's front door. When would you be able to do that by?
Jack	I could do it within the next two weeks.
Me	Tim, is that OK with you?
Tim	Yes, that's fine.
Me	Great, let's put a date on that. So two weeks from today is the fourth of April, so shall I write 'Jack agrees to re-paint Tim's front door by the fourth of April'?
Jack and Tim	Yes.
Jack	Hang on. Tim, you need to get the paint in time for me to do that.
Me	Tim, how would you like to incorporate that into agreement?

Tim	How about we say that I'll have the paint available in two days' time and then Jack can do the painting any time within the next two weeks?
Me	Jack, is that OK with you?
Jack	Sounds good.
Me	So shall I write 'Tim will get the paint by Thursday this week and Jack will re-paint the front door of Tim's house by the fourth of April'?
Jack and Tim	Yes, that'll do.

I will write this down and go through similar steps with the remaining terms. Once both Tim and Jack are satisfied, I read out the whole agreement to ensure both are still happy with what's written. Each signs this Settlement Agreement.

Once things are completed, I thank them again, remind them about confidentiality, discuss any follow-up steps and wave them off into the sunset.

If Tim and Jack were not able to reach agreement, I would bring the mediation to a close at an appropriate point. I thank them for trying, advise of next steps, reinforce confidentiality more strongly and then escort them to the exit individually.

This mediation will have lasted from as little as an hour to as long as ten hours, depending on the nature of the dispute.

Outcome of mediation

There are a number of potential outcomes to mediation. The meeting could end with:

1. A written agreement covering all the issues between the parties with the terms fulfilled there and then. For example, 'Fred apologies to Myrtle for being a plonker and agrees to pay her £100 compensation for digging up her flower bed'. Fred hands over £100 in cash.
2. A written agreement covering all the issues between the parties with some terms yet to be fulfilled. 'Fred apologies to Myrtle and agrees that he will buy new plants for her flower bed and put them in within the next two weeks (by 4 April).'
3. A written agreement covering some, but not all, of the issues between the parties. 'Fred will buy new plants for Myrtle's

flower bed by 4 April to replace those he dug up. The parties have not resolved their differences about who broke the fence and recognise that Myrtle may decide to continue with her court action on this matter.'

4. A Memorandum of Understanding recording where matters stand at the end of the mediation. 'Myrtle will find out how much it will cost to rebuild the greenhouse and the replacement cost of the exotic plants from the Himalayas. Fred recognises that he may be liable for some of the damage caused, but the extent of this liability will be discussed once the relevant costs are known. Myrtle will keep Fred informed if it is taking longer than a month from today to find out the costs.'

Or: 'The parties agree that Myrtle will not pay rent to Fred for lease of the commercial premises of the greenhouse until the costs of repair of the building and the replacement of the exotic plants are known and agreed, and the premises and vegetation are back to the state they were in before the damage was caused. The parties agree that their solicitors will draft a Settlement Agreement to reflect this Memorandum of Understanding by 30 April latest and that each party will sign the Agreement within seven days of the terms being accepted.'

5. A verbal agreement resolving all issues:

Fred   Myrtle, I'm really sorry that I destroyed the flower bed after coming back from the pub. It won't happen again, because I realise it was a stupid thing to do. Here's £100 to cover the cost of replacing the plants.

Myrtle   OK, I accept your apology. I realise it was not like you to have done this damage. I'll use the money to put in some new plants in the spring.

6. A verbal agreement resolving some of the issues. *Not* a good idea. If the outcome of the mediation is that there is partial agreement, it is far better to put this in writing. The parties' recollections of events have a funny habit of being completely different within a short time after mediation when the agreement is not in writing.

7. No agreement reached on the issues in dispute.

Later in this book, we consider your role as a lawyer in the documentation and aftermath of these potential outcomes.

Sometimes I am asked how I define a successful mediation. From a statistical standpoint, the easiest way is to say that if there has been a written agreement which results in all the issues being resolved, then that mediation is successful. Hence the oft-quoted success rate of around 80 per cent.

From a practical viewpoint, a mediation may be regarded as successful if it managed to narrow the issues between the parties, thus reducing the amount of time spent in court. It may also be successful in the eyes of one party if he realises there is no point pursuing the other side further because the dispute is not as black and white as he originally thought – a case of 'No point in wasting any more time on this – let's just move on with life'.

Whether your client regards the mediation as 'successful' will to a large extent depend on how you as his adviser and how the mediator manage his expectations. More on this in Chapter 6.

Summary

- Mediation can be used in a wide range of situations, and you could always be the first to introduce it to a new area.
- It's suitable for your commercial clients and your family law clients, and for schools, in the workplace, for complaints, and even for shipping.
- Sometimes, though, it is not appropriate – need for precedent, an unwilling party, the requirement for an injunction, public interest, vexatious litigants, or a power imbalance.
- The process of mediation is fairly standard, but the flow is flexible to meet the needs of the parties.
- Parties such as your client retain control of the outcome.
- The outcome may be written or verbal. There may be complete or partial agreement or none at all.
- Any outcome could be regarded as a 'success'; it just depends who's looking at it and for what purpose.

Notes

1. Acland, *A Sudden Outbreak of Commonsense*: 2.
2. Phillips and Ignacio, 'Entertainment industry'.
3. Newman, 'A creative industry'.
4. *O'Neill.*

5. NHS Litigation Authority, *Clinical Disputes Forum's Guide*.
6. Legal Ombudsman Scheme Rules, section 5.17.
7. Legal Ombudsman Business Plan 2010, p. 7.
8. *Mediation Leaflet*.
9. NHS Litigation Authority, *Clinical Dispute Forum's Users' Guide*.
10. Patient Rights (Scotland) Act 2011, s. 15 (5).
11. *Faidi*, para. 35.
12. Ibid., para.37.
13. *Oliver*, para. 1.
14. Rozee and Powell, *Mediation in Planning*.
15. Ibid., p. 62. (See also p. 63 for the solicitor's comments on the process.)
16. Gould and others, *The Use of Mediation in Construction Disputes*.
17. Ibid., p. 32.
18. Gould, King and Britton, *Mediating Construction Disputes*.
19. Agapiou and Clark, *An Investigation of Construction Lawyer Attitudes*.
20. *Daniels*.

Chapter 4

'SELLING' MEDIATION

Scenario One

The scene	Ages and ages ago
The cast	Ugg – a caveman
	Blango – a flash git from the other side of the mountain
Blango	Greetings Ugg! Haven't seen you for many winters. How are things with you?
Ugg [moaning]	Oh, same old routine. Get up in the morning, put on my goatskin and head out to try to find some breakfast. Wear myself out trying to find something to kill and then have to try to drag the stupid beast back to my cave. Feeding my fifteen kids is a real hassle these days.
Blango	I tell you what. You should buy this new thing I've invented. I've called it a 'wheel'. You can have it for twenty goats and two of your wives.
Ugg (furious)	Twenty goats and two wives! You've got to be joking. I can't afford that. I'm supporting a large family and life isn't getting any easier. You can take your wheel and . . .

Scenario Two

The scene	Ages and ages ago
The cast	Ugg – a caveman
	Blango – a flash git from the other side of the mountain
Blango	Greetings Ugg! Haven't seen you for many winters. How are things with you?
Ugg [moaning]	Oh, same old routine. Get up in the morning, put on my goatskin and head out to try to find some breakfast. Wear myself out trying to find something to kill and then have to try to drag

	the stupid beast back to my cave. Feeding my fifteen kids is a real hassle these days.
Blango	It's difficult trying to feed so many mouths. Looks as though all your children are starting to grow up fast, too. Are their appetites out of control yet?
Ugg	You should see them! All they seem to do all day is eat and lie around in the cave while I'm out there lugging animals around. My back is killing me and the soles of my feet are cut from walking on sharp stones all the time.
Blango	How will you cope if your back gives out on you or you can't walk long distances any more?
Ugg	It'd be a disaster. None of the kids is big enough to haul a dead bison back here for dinner. We wouldn't have food to eat. We'd be doomed!
Blango	If I could offer you a solution which would help you have enough to eat, would you be interested?
Ugg	Too right I would!
Blango	I've invented something which you could attach to a box. You put the bison into the box, and it takes hardly any effort to haul it back to the cave to feed everyone. I've called it a 'wheel'. It's round, so that means it's easy to move.
Ugg	Sounds like the sort of thing I need. How much is it?
Blango	You can have it for twenty goats and two wives.
Ugg	H'mm, that's not bad. You've got a deal. I'll take two.

What's happened here? In Scenario One, our caveman has adamantly refused to consider buying a wheel. In the second, though, he's totally convinced and buys two.

Blango's first attempt to convince Ugg of the benefits of a wheel has fallen flat as he has failed to think about what's important to his customer. Blango knows what a wheel is and understands how helpful it can be. Ugg has never seen a wheel in action and thinks that this flash git is just trying to make money out of him.

In Scenario Two, Blango has taken a little time to understand Ugg's situation and the problems he's facing. Once he has asked Ugg to think about a potential worst-case scenario, Blango then offers a solution which his customer readily accepts.

This approach is referred to as SPIN® Selling, a concept developed by Huthwaite Inc.[1] The concept behind it is that once a potential customer recognises the implication of his problem and sees how the product or service can directly benefit him, he is more likely to buy. How does this work? The term 'SPIN®' refers to the type of questions asked. While this book doesn't go into depth on this topic, let me explain it briefly:

S – Situation – 'How are things with you?'

P – Problem – 'Are their appetites out of control yet?'

I – Implication – 'How will you cope if you can't walk long distances any more?'

N – Need – 'If I could offer you a solution which would help you have enough to eat, would you be interested?'

Benefits of mediation

When Blango was talking to Ugg in Scenario Two, he touched on the benefits of the wheel. Once you fit it onto the box, 'it takes hardly any effort to haul [the bison] back to the cave', and because the wheel is round, 'it's easy to move'.

So what are the benefits of mediation? They are:

1. Time
   a. Not only can mediations usually be arranged fairly quickly, they are generally shorter than court proceedings or protracted negotiations.
   b. The length of mediations varies. If the parties are not paying a fee (for example, court-sponsored mediations, complaints made through a public body), the meeting may be restricted to, say, 2–3 hours.
   c. Family mediations may involve a number of meetings of 1–1½ hours over a number of weeks.
   d. Workplace mediations tend to last around seven hours.
   e. Commercial mediations will go for at least a day, and in my experience this is the norm. However, if the dispute involves complex issues, or if a number of parties are participating,

they may last longer. If the parties have been in dispute for a number of years, it may be unrealistic to assume that everything will be sorted with a day's mediation. For a longer mediation, subsequent meetings may be on consecutive days or spread out over a period of time.

(For those who are self-employed or for professionals such as lawyers, time spent in negotiations or waiting outside the courtroom is time when they could be earning money. For them, mediation may be an attractive option to consider.

Also, many disputes seem to run on forever, with the parties reluctant or refusing to really focus on the issues. The joy of mediation is that when people know they have, say, a day to try to resolve matters, they usually do. They've come along voluntarily, the mediator has set a positive tone for resolution, and the parties see the meeting as an opportunity to sort things out once and for all.)

2. Cost
   a. One of the benefits of mediation over litigation is that the costs are usually known in advance.
   b. The mediator has quoted a fee and advised the parties of the venue and catering costs, so everyone knows how much they will be paying.
   c. Costs tend to be lower than those incurred through more formal processes.
   d. Mediation is cost-effective, though this doesn't necessarily mean cheap. As the research into the use of mediation in construction disputes found, 'the higher the costs of the mediation itself, the greater the cost savings going forward'.[2]
   e. Lost opportunity costs are minimised. This is particularly important for many commercial clients. If a dispute drags on for months or years, the key players in the company tend to take their eyes off the business while they worry about the conflict. The longer this is happening, the more business opportunities may come and go without being recognised and taken up. Mediation shortens the length of time before potential resolution, so the management team can get back to business quickly.

3. Confidentiality
   a. This principle of mediation is one which many clients regard as a huge benefit.
   b. Commercial clients like the opportunity to try to resolve disputes in private. They potentially avoid adverse publicity or the need to reveal proprietary information in a public forum.
   c. For professionals – such as doctors and lawyers – who are facing a complaint made against them, the confidential nature of mediation reassures them that they can make an apology without fear of creating further liability.
   d. When disputes between employees come to mediation, confidentiality allows each to discuss personal matters which may have exacerbated the conflict in the working relationship.
4. Control
   a. The parties control when the mediation takes place and how long it will last.
   b. The parties retain control of the outcome. They don't have to agree to anything they don't choose to.
   c. The terms of the Settlement Agreement can be ones which no court or tribunal could dictate. For example, the parties can devise payment terms which suit them, agree to undertake specific actions or set out ground rules for working together in the future.

When you are reading the next sections about 'selling', I suggest you keep these benefits in mind. When 'selling' mediation, think about which one or ones of these benefits may be attractive to your audience.

'Selling' mediation to your client

Let's look at a simple example. A client has come to you seeking advice about a customer's failure to pay her bill of £10,000. In your opinion, mediation is a suitable dispute resolution method in this case:

Scenario One
You   I gather you installed a new bathroom for Mr Brown, and that he still owes you ten thousand pounds.

Client	That's right. I want to sue the b*****d and get my money back.
You	What about trying mediation rather than court? It's faster and the discussions are confidential.
Client	No, I don't like the idea of that. I want everyone to know what this bloke's like. Just because he's some smart City type, he can't get away with not paying people like me. His sort always thinks that we won't chase them because we can't afford it. This is not just about the money – it's a point of principle.
	Some time later . . .
You	'We are pleased to submit our fee note . . .'
Client	I'm not paying that. You said that if we won, the Court would award me expenses. How come I'm out of pocket?

Scenario Two using the SPIN® Selling approach:

You	How did this money become payable to you? [situation]
Client	He'd agreed to pay me to install a new bathroom for him.
You	How's this affecting your cash flow? [problem]
Client	Things are really tight at the moment and I've got a large tax bill to pay next month.
You	What might happen to your business without this ten thousand pounds? [implication]
Client	I'd have to lay off Bob, who's been working with me for twenty years.
You	If I could help you keep Bob on, would you be interested? [need]
Client	Too right I would!
You	Let me tell you about the option of mediation . . .

What you've done here is focus your client's mind on to the possibility of having to sack Bob, rather than on the £10,000. Once you've done this, your client is likely to be open to ways of saving Bob's job and willing to consider mediation.

> **Sidebar**
>
> It may be, though, that your client still doesn't understand what you are getting at. The reason for this may be that she prefers to absorb new information in a different way.
>
> While this book does not go into the depths of communication styles, other writers, such as Fleming,[3] suggest that we each have a preferred way of learning (and taking in information – my addition) –by seeing, by hearing or by doing. Advertisers recognise this and often join elements so that they can target a wider audience. Think about television ads. They may include something quirky like a grouse doing aerobics to capture the attention of those who prefer *seeing* new ideas. Along with that visual, there will be a catchy tune for those of us who prefer *hearing*. And what about 'opening offers' or discounts? The purpose of those is to tempt us to experience the product or service for ourselves by *doing* or *using* it.

The reason for including this sidebar is to encourage you to think of different ways of conveying the message of mediation to your client. When I managed the Edinburgh Sheriff Court Mediation Service, I developed the diagram below (Figure 4.1) to show the options to parties. Many of them, once they could see that a court action wouldn't necessarily be over in a one-hour episode as it is on television, recognised one of the advantages of mediation. You may like to create something similar and relevant for your jurisdiction for your own use.

'Selling' mediation to the other party's solicitor

In the past, some lawyers may have felt that to suggest mediation was a sign of weakness.[4] However, research undertaken by The Law Society of New South Wales in Australia shows that practitioners who have used mediation have identified a number of benefits,[5] including:

- improvement in legal practitioner/client relations through the provision of an appropriate forum for the parties to make decisions, as opposed to hasty settlements made on the court steps . . .
- early recoupment of costs and funded disbursements.

These are just two of the benefits you could think about when approaching the other party's solicitor. In addition, there are the

Court procedure

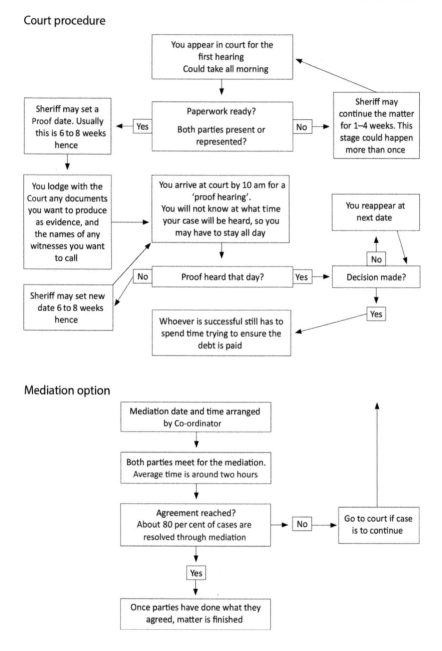

Mediation option

Figure 4.1   Options for dispute resolution

practical points where you may both have been exchanging letters for quite some time, no one is budging and frankly you're all starting to get frustrated. It's like the saying 'If you keep doing what you've always done, you'll keep getting what you've always got'. Perhaps it's time to try something different.

Maybe the response from the other side is that it won't be possible to sort anything, because of one particular point about which her client is adamant. That's fine – why not consider mediation to try to narrow the issues? There may then be agreement on some points. If the dispute is going to end up in court, at least you'll spend less time there as the number of matters requiring a judgment will be fewer.

Using the SPIN® approach again, consider what the other client may be really concerned about when suggesting mediation to his lawyer. For example:

You	What's your client's main concern about sorting out this dispute?
Other solicitor	He's told me that it's all taking too long to resolve.
You	How is the delay affecting him?
OS	Well, I obviously can't breach confidentiality, but like most clients he is probably concerned that the costs are mounting up.
You	If that were his concern, how do you think he will react if the costs are substantial?
OS	He'd be annoyed because the amount in dispute is not that great. We'd probably look at reducing our fee a bit to keep him onside.
You	If I could suggest an option which might resolve matters quickly and help you charge your entire fee, would you be interested?
OS	Bring it on!

Solicitors must act in the best interests of their clients, but as it is the lawyer with whom you are having this conversation, it is important to make the option of mediation a positive one for her too.

If the other solicitor has had little experience of mediation, it may be helpful to suggest she talk to a mediator. On a number of occasions, I have been called by a firm who is keen to mediate but aren't sure how to convince the other side. They ask me if I would be willing to talk to the other solicitor about the process. Of course I would. They give the other solicitor my telephone number so that it is up to her to make contact. I can then have an informal chat about the process, answer any questions and leave the other solicitor with good information to discuss with her client.

If you are writing to the other solicitor, rather than speaking on the phone I suggest you construct your letter along similar lines to the conversation above. For example:

> We understand from previous correspondence that your client is keen to resolve matters quickly. Our client would like a speedy resolution too and we are keen to keep her outlays as low as possible.
>
> To this end we have looked at options which can be arranged quickly and which have reasonable costs. It would seem that mediation may be in the best interests of both our clients.
>
> We have spoken informally to a mediator, who says she could organise a mediation date within the next few weeks if that suited everyone. She has advised that the cost for the mediation would be £xxx. We suggest that this be split 50/50 between our clients.
>
> If you would be interested in finding out more about the actual process of mediation, [mediator] is more than happy to talk to you about it on the phone and to answer any questions you may have. Her number is [xxx].
>
> We await your response to our suggestion.

Sidebar

Before one mediation, I spoke on the phone to a party who was a highly experienced businessman. While he had taken his solicitor's advice to participate in mediation, he was still fairly cynical about the process. His opening comments to me were along the lines of 'I always go to court and I always win'.

We had a mediation lasting around nine hours. It resulted in an agreement that satisfied both parties and which was drawn up by the parties' solicitors before everyone left.

Part of the businessman's feedback to me after the mediation was that the experience was very worthwhile and better than the sometimes illogical outcomes of court.

'Selling' mediation to your firm or partners

Solicitors who have many years of experience may be sceptical about using mediation if they feel it is taking income away from the firm. Their resistance may be strong in spite of the benefit of retaining good clients, and the duty to act in the best interests of the client. What they may not have realised is that the appropriate use of mediation gives your firm the opportunity to keep one client happy while undertaking work for another at the same time.

What do I mean by this? Let's take the example of our bathroom installer who is owed £10,000. Let's call her Ann. She's a longstanding client for whom you have set up a business partnership and acted when she bought her first house, and you have also helped her with her will – all good run-of-the-mill work. You know, though, that your fees for trying to recover the £10,000 could be substantial, and after listening to your advice she's agreed to participate in mediation. Through your correspondence with the other party's solicitor, you have gained their agreement too and the parties have decided on the mediator. You've helped Ann prepare properly for the meeting so there is no need for you to attend the mediation itself. While the mediation is taking place, you are carrying out work for another client.

After the mediation, Ann contacts you to advise that she's very happy with the outcome as she has reached an agreement with the other party. When you send her your fee note for the work you've done, she pays promptly and adds a note thanking you for fixing the problem so quickly. Satisfied client who is likely to tell others how good you are at what you do (remember Chapter 1).

So why does the use of mediation in this instance benefit your firm? Not only have you maintained a good relationship with a client, your firm has been paid promptly and you've been earning additional fees by doing other work while the mediation takes place.

If you do attend the mediation with your client, you have presumably both made the decision that your presence would be beneficial. Of course, your client is paying your fee for this, but at the end of the meeting, you are more than likely to have cemented your business relationship with her. While this book doesn't discuss the cost of gaining new clients, in other types of business it is always far cheaper to retain a good client than to have to find a new one to replace the disgruntled.

Summary

- SPIN® doesn't always have negative, 'political' implications.
- Twenty goats and two wives is a bargain when you can see that a wheel will make life easier.
- When 'selling' mediation, consider who you are addressing and adapt your approach to fit.
- The appropriate use of mediation benefits your client, the other party and your business.
- Your clients are unlikely to thank you if their cost has exceeded the value of the claim.

Notes

1. <www.huthwaite.com>
2. Gould and others, *The Use of Mediation in Construction Disputes*.
3. Fleming and Mills, *Not Another Inventory*.
4. Peters and Mastin, 'To mediate or not to mediate'.
5. Law Society of New South Wales, *Dispute Resolution Kit*: 7.

Chapter 5

CHOOSING A MEDIATOR

The next logical step is to choose a mediator. However, logic sometimes isn't always so straightforward. While the previous chapter was all about convincing others of the benefits of mediation, how do you convince yourself? Until you've either experienced mediation yourself or have heard of its success from a trusted colleague, how can you be sure that you're making the right suggestion to your client? Part of the self-reassurance is feeling confident in the abilities of the mediators you may recommend. So which do you do first? Find a mediator you trust, or convince your client to try mediation and then hunt around?

Let's assume that you've never used mediation before but are open to the idea. A client, Nick, comes to you with a problem about property subsidence in the commercial premises which he leases from Ella, the owner. The back part of the shop collapsed because of water damage, which seems to have been caused by poor maintenance of the drainage system. There was considerable damage to Nick's stock and the business has been closed for three months while repairs are undertaken by Ella. The contract between the parties clearly shows that the owner is responsible for the maintenance, but Ella seems to be slow to do the repair work. Nick wants to 'do something' to make Ella hurry up and then to compensate him for loss of stock and business.

You've read the early chapters of this book, so you think that mediation might be an appropriate option here. You don't want to jeopardise your relationship with your client by suggesting something you haven't experienced before and then having it all go pear-shaped. Your conversation with Nick could be along the following lines:

You	So the shop's been closed for the past three months and Ella's been slow doing the repair work. [situation]
Nick	Yes, I want to get open again, and for her to compensate me for my losses.
You	What's your main concern about the delay? [problem]
Nick	Without the cash flow I'm struggling to keep up with my loan commitments.

You	If you fail to make the payments, what's the penalty? [implication]
Nick	The bank's unlikely to call my loan in straightaway because I've been a loyal customer, but they could make it difficult for me to extend my overdraft.
You	If we could work out a speedy way to resolve this, would that help you keep the repayments going? [need]
Nick	Definitely.
You	There's an option which may suit you – mediation. In brief, it's where you and Ella would have the opportunity to sit down together with an impartial facilitator to sort things out quickly. I've heard lots of good reports from my colleagues about mediation but I haven't had the chance to try it yet. How about I make some calls to check that this would be the best option for you? Once I know some more, we can discuss it and see if mediation would be the fastest way to keep those loan repayments flowing.
Nick	You're a star!

What to look for

I suggest that you find out the names of some mediators, call each of them, and talk through the issue with them.[1]

Personal assessment

The most important purpose of this call is for you make an initial assessment of the mediator. What you really want to know is whether this person will work well with Nick so that, as your client, he feels reassured that you have acted in his best interests.

Sidebar

An article by McKnight and others[2] discusses the ways in which initial trust is established in new relationships. In the same journal, Lewicki, McAllister and Bies refer to the narrow bandwidth at the start of relationships. Within this, an initial trust may develop, and the authors go on to say:

> In interpersonal relationships of trust and distrust, we see potential for enlargement in relationship bandwidth as partners accumulate knowledge of each other's strengths and/or weaknesses in new interaction domains.[3]
>
> For me, these articles paint an exact picture of the challenge facing mediators, who must draw on their experience to instil confidence in parties from their initial interaction. A good mediator is able to do this. As the relationship develops, the parties feel more confident in the mediator's ability to help them listen to each other and discuss issues effectively. So in your initial call to the mediator, you want to start to assess her ability to build trust.

Here are some points to be aware of. Does the mediator:

1. Establish rapport quickly with you?
    a. This is a key sign of a good mediator. For example, she must be astute enough to tune into your wavelength, your way of speaking, and your use of language. If you feel rushed by the mediator, it may be that your mode of speech is slow and hers is fast and she has failed to pick up on this difference. If that is happening during a phone call, how might your client feel during mediation? How might the slight discord that you feel with the mediator show itself in your discussions with your client?
    b. The reason rapport building is an essential skill is that it is the basis for building trust between the mediator and the parties. Your client may be revealing things to a complete stranger; he needs to feel comfortable that this person will not pass judgement on his actions or opinions.
2. Listen carefully to what you are saying?
    a. Mediators should be skilled listeners. If you feel that she is jumping to conclusions about what you say, interrupting or perhaps trying to provide you with an instant solution, the warning bells should ring.
    b. A good mediator will listen carefully to what you're telling her and understand the reasons for your call. She will ask appropriate questions and will refrain from commenting on the merits or otherwise of your client's case.

    c. The reason this is so important is that during mediation the mediator should talk far less than everyone else. It is her role to listen to what each person is saying and when appropriate summarise, re-frame and clarify. Remember it will be the parties' meeting, not the mediator's. If indications on the phone are that the mediator thinks what she has to say is more important than what you are telling her, listen to that bell.

3. Decline the work if she is not appropriately trained?

    a. Lots of people have been trained as mediators, usually in a specific area. Simply because she is an experienced family mediator doesn't mean that she will be helpful in a commercial dispute such as Nick's. A good mediator will tell you immediately if she is not trained in the dispute area you are calling about. She should advise you of that and give you contact details of mediators or organisations who may better meet your client's needs.

    b. The reason for this is that while the basic skill set is the same, the approach needed is usually different.[4] For example, a commercial mediation may last a day whereas a family one may stretch over a number of weeks or months. In this situation, the meetings may be shorter with the mediator working with the parties separately. A mediator who is used to that approach may not be suitable for the intensity of a full-on day of discussion. It's just like you as a lawyer, perhaps knowing something about wills and trusts, but having far more experience in litigation.

4. Decline the work if she does not feel capable of undertaking it?

    a. This is always a difficult one for a mediator. She's done the training and is raring to go. She doesn't want to pass up an opportunity to try out her new skills. However, you might not want your client to be her guinea pig. An honest mediator will tell you that she's 'just starting out' or that she hasn't 'done a mediation as big as this sounds before'. You can then delve deeper to find out whether you are willing to give her a chance.

    b. The reason this is so important is that it goes again to the development of trust and to the credibility of the mediator. If you find out too late that the mediator is not capable, your client will not thank you.

   c. The good mediator will tell you of her limited experience or lack of experience. She may recommend someone else, or she may ask if she can talk to a fellow mediator about the dispute (without breaching confidentiality, of course). If you agree, then the first mediator may suggest to her colleague that they work in tandem so that she gains experience. There should be no extra charge for having two mediators in an instance such as this. The parties benefit because they have the 'right' mediator, and two heads for the price of one.

5. Check for any conflict of interest?

   a. The mediator should advise you if she knows any of the parties or lawyers involved in the dispute.

   b. The reason the mediator should disclose this is to demonstrate that she is honest and trustworthy. As was mentioned earlier, one of the cornerstones of mediation is the impartiality of the mediator. The last thing anyone needs is for a party or lawyer to greet the mediator as an old friend at the start of the meeting.

   c. Don't be surprised, though, if the mediator doesn't ask you for the names of the parties at the start of your phone call to her. Initially it may be that both of you prefer to discuss the situation without mentioning the names of those in dispute. This anonymity allows you to feel comfortable about talking to a mediator you may not have met.

   d. My approach is to wait until the lawyer and I have had a general chat about the situation. It's only when it gets to the stage of 'Would you mind talking to my client about the process?' that I ask for the names of all involved. Sometimes the first call from the lawyer may not reach that stage. In such instances, before the end of the conversation, I may say something like 'If you would like to take this further, I must ensure I don't have a conflict of interest. So when you come back to me, it would be helpful if you could let me know the names of the parties and lawyers so I can make sure I don't know them well. Is that OK?'

   e. However, the mere fact that people know each other does not automatically preclude this mediator. The most important thing is that everyone involved is informed of the relationship and that each has agreed that he or she is prepared to work with that mediator. In my experience, it is becoming increasingly difficult to work with lawyers I haven't met before. I now make it quite clear that if anyone expresses concern that my impartiality may be compromised, I will step aside from being the mediator.

6. Explain the process of mediation clearly?

   a. The mediator must be able to tell you about the process and key principles in a way that is easy to understand. She should answer your questions to your satisfaction.

   b. If you feel confused by what the mediator is telling you and if she doesn't clarify your concerns, then this may not be the person to recommend to your client.

   c. When parties come to mediation they are usually stepping into the unknown. The mediator has to be able to explain clearly how the day may flow and what the ground rules are, and to give the parties a sense of what lies ahead. (One of the worst examples I have seen was a mediator who at the start of the meeting skipped the small talk, rattled off the 'rules', gave no opportunity for questions, and then launched straight into asking the parties to tell *him* what the dispute was all about. Wrong, wrong, wrong. This was almost as bad as the lawyer who, as mediator, said to the parties 'I put it to you . . .')

7. Discuss the pros and cons of mediation with you?

   a. Mediators are generally passionate advocates of their profession. This is great, but if you feel that the mediator is being *too* enthusiastic, then it may be worth asking more questions.

   b. A good mediator will have listened to what you've said and then will have explained any downside of mediation. For example:

You	There have been a number of grievances lodged against this manager already. He's been told he has to go to mediation so things can be sorted out.
Mediator	Remember, mediation is voluntary, so if the manager is being forced to participate the chances of things being sorted out could be pretty low. It could well be a waste of time and money for mediation to be attempted.

8. Demonstrate that she knows how to arrange the logistics?
   a. The logistics are important because they add to the reassurance of all involved. You should feel that the mediator will take care of any venue and catering arrangements needed, and not you, unless that's your choice.
   b. The mediator should explain what documentation she will send out before the meeting and what she would ideally like to receive from the parties. Of course, this discussion may not happen in your first phone call, but it's all part of helping you sum up the capabilities of the mediator. If she sounds chaotic about arrangements, it doesn't bode well for the mediation itself.
9. Offer to have an informal chat about the process with your client and/or the other party's lawyer?
   a. There is, of course, no obligation for a mediator to offer to do this. However, to me it makes sense. In the UK, lawyers and parties are still getting used to mediation and there are often questions to be answered and processes explained.
   b. The mediator should not charge you for this. If she says she will, you may not feel comfortable recommending a mediator who seems to want to charge for every preliminary phone call.
10. Offer to send you further information?
    a. This is simple courtesy. Even if the mediator realises that you are not likely to use her services in this particular instance, a smart one will offer to send information to keep her name in sight. Again it goes to professionalism.
    b. If you get the feeling that there is a reluctance to send you anything until you sign on the dotted line (or if she doesn't have anything to send you), this may help you decide whether to recommend this mediator or not.
    c. The material doesn't have to be a glossy brochure. The most important thing is that is readily understandable.
11. Provide you with a clear pricing structure?
    a. Usually when a lawyer contacts me in the first instance, it is to find out information so he can convey this to his client. Part of this is the potential cost. Even though the extent of the mediation may not be completely clear at this stage, the mediator should be able to tell you how she prices her services.

  b. Some charge by the hour, some by the day or by the meet-
     ing. It doesn't matter which, but what is essential is that you
     have a good idea of how much your client may be up for.
     For example, at Mediation Scotland, we have fixed price
     bands for most work so are able to quote a price per party
     for a day's mediation, and to give an estimate of venue and
     catering costs.
  c. The pricing structure is important to know. You don't want
     to have convinced all involved that mediation is the way to
     go and then find that the costs are very much more than you
     originally thought. This doesn't help your credibility.

Subject matter expertise

It is not essential that the mediator has industry or technical expertise in the subject matter of the dispute. In fact, it's often better if she
doesn't. The reason for this is that it ensures she doesn't fall into the
trap of making assumptions about the opinions of the parties and
cross the line of impartiality. A good mediator will prepare thoroughly so that she understands the terminology of the sector. During
the meeting the parties should not have to spend time helping the
mediator understand terms which they already know themselves.

However, in complex matters where two mediators are needed,
this may change. For example, if the mediation is about a shipping
dispute and substantial sums of money are at stake, it may be best to
have a lead mediator without shipping knowledge. The co-mediator
could have this expertise and use it to assist the lead person in facili-
tating the discussion.

Quality assurance

One of the difficulties for mediation as a profession in the UK is that
there is no single accrediting body. Anyone who has undergone mediation training (and even some who haven't) can call herself a 'mediator'. So if you are still not certain about a particular mediator or are
not able to refer to an accrediting body, ask her:

  1. How many hours of initial training did she undertake? It
     should be at least 30 hours, include role-plays and formal
     assessment, and have been delivered by an experienced media-
     tor and trainer.

2. After passing the training, how much time has she spent co-mediating with someone more experienced? It should be at least six hours and two mediations.

3. How much time does she spend each year on continuing professional development? This should be a minimum of 12 hours and may include peer and personal review, additional training, or mentoring.

4. Which code of conduct does she operate under? There are a number of different ones, but in essence they are all the same. Whichever she names, it should be in line with the European Code of Conduct for Mediators.[5]

5. What complaints procedure does she have in place? She should have a written process which is readily available to anyone who asks.

6. What level of professional indemnity insurance does she have? If the answer is 'none', ask why. A professional mediator will have a minimum of £1,000,000 cover, with a follow-on so that if a claim is made against her after she has ceased trading, the policy can be called upon.

Sidebar

A good mediator should offer sensible advice about the choice of venue. Usually it is best if the meeting is held on neutral ground. This ensures that one party does not have a psychological advantage of being on home territory. However, many lawyers have excellent meeting-room facilities, so it can save costs to use these. If you offer this accommodation to the mediator, she should tell you that she will speak to the other party to see if he agrees to this. If your client is the one approached, the mediator should ensure that no pressure is brought to bear to make him feel he has to accept the suggested venue.

Lawyers as mediators

When helping your client choose a mediator, you may be attracted by the idea of suggesting a fellow legal practitioner to fulfil the role. In my view, this can pose some difficulties.

Firstly, it is often hard for qualified mediators to build up experience once they are accredited. It is like the problem that school leavers or graduates often have – they can't get a job without experience in the area, but no one will employ them because they don't have experience. For legal practitioners whose time is consumed by the day job, it may be even more problematic to undertake enough mediations to build their confidence and expertise. Acting as a mediator is like any skill – you have to keep practising, otherwise you lose your edge. A lawyer who does the occasional mediation may not be the best choice for your client.

Secondly, there is the concern that parties are unable to differentiate between the 'lawyer' and the 'mediator'. Remember that most people have not experienced mediation before. The whole situation is new to them. They may still think it is part of the 'formal legal process'. I have frequently encountered parties who ask me for advice or for a legal opinion – and I'm not a practising lawyer. I have to remind them that my role is to be independent and that I am not qualified to practise law in Scotland. Mostly, this latter comment ensures they do not press me further. However, it could prove difficult if the lawyer is qualified to practise in the jurisdiction.

Some jurisdictions have particular rules relating to lawyers acting as mediators. For example, the American Bar Association rule about lawyers serving as a third-party neutral states:

> A lawyer serving as a third-party neutral shall inform unrepresented parties that the lawyer is not representing them. When the lawyer knows or reasonably should know that a party does not understand the lawyer's role in the matter, the lawyer shall explain the difference between the lawyer's role as a third-party neutral and a lawyer's role as one who represents a client.[6]

The Law Society of New South Wales in Australia has comprehensive guidelines for legal practitioners who act as mediators. These seek to ensure that 'different hats' are quite clear. For example, in Clause 5.1, when referring to impartiality, part of the guideline reminds practitioners that 'The mediator shall not play an adversarial role'.[7] Clause 5.4 further clarifies the importance of impartiality: 'a mediator who is a business partner or an associate of any legal counsel retained by either of the parties should not act as mediator.'[8]

Of course, I am not asserting that there are no good mediators who are also practising lawyers. All I am highlighting is that when you are helping your clients choose a mediator, it might be an idea to keep these concerns in mind.

Summary

A good mediator:

- Builds rapport quickly
- Listens to you, explains clearly, answers questions satisfactorily
- Says if she thinks she shouldn't undertake the work
- Tells you if she thinks mediation is not appropriate for the dispute
- Goes the extra mile and is well-organised
- Leaves you feeling that you trust her and comfortable about recommending her to your client

Check her credentials:

- Has she undertaken at least 30 hours' initial training?
- Has she worked with a more experienced mediator after the training?
- Does she undertake ongoing CPD?
- Does she operate under a suitable code of conduct?
- Does she have a complaints procedure?
- Does she have adequate insurance?

Most importantly, if she doesn't 'feel right' to you, she will probably not be right for your client.

See Appendix 7 for a suggested checklist for choosing a mediator

Notes

1. The best way to locate a mediator is through word of mouth. Otherwise an internet search is likely to provide the most current information.
2. McKnight and others, 'Initial trust formation'.
3. Lewicki and others, 'Trust and distrust'.
4. See Appendix 17 for more information about different styles of mediation.
5. See Appendix 19.
6. Model Rules of Professional Conduct, Rule 2.4 (b).
7. Law Society of New South Wales, *Dispute Resolution Kit*.
8. Ibid.

Chapter 6

ROLE OF THE LEGAL PRACTITIONER

Once the parties have agreed to mediate and have chosen a mediator, you take on other roles with your client in the next stages – preparation, during the mediation, follow-up afterwards. The first and most important step is to help your client with thorough preparation so she can make the informed decisions at mediation. The second stage arises if you are present at the mediation with your client. You are there to support her, the mediator and the process. In the final stage (post-mediation), your role may involve ensuring that settlement terms have been fulfilled. You should also take the opportunity to cement the relationship with your client and reflect on the mediation itself. Let's consider these roles chronologically.

Preparing for mediation

In my experience, one of the main factors contributing to a successful mediation is good preparation by all concerned. The preparation phase has three parts – what you have to prepare to guide your client, what your client should prepare herself and what you need to do jointly. The sad reality, though, is that many lawyers fail to prepare their clients properly. They may touch on the chances of success/failure in court and the potential costs of litigation, but neglect to discuss the impact of an ongoing dispute on the client's business and the personal stress for those involved.

Failure to prepare properly also puts your client in a weak negotiating position during the mediation. In an article[1] about ADR in employment situations, David Trevor reinforces the need for lawyers to be properly prepared before arbitration or mediation. While the scenarios of employment mediations may not be the same as those in your jurisdiction, the points about lawyer preparation remain valid and valuable.

Help your clients prepare for the mediation – whether you are going to attend the meeting with them or not. The client who is well-prepared understands the strengths and weaknesses of her own case and of the other party's. She has relevant documents at her finger-tips with copies for others if appropriate; she has ensured that other advisers (for example, accountants) are either at the mediation with her or are readily available at the end of the phone if needed. Overall, the client makes better decisions because they are *informed* decisions.

There are a number of tools to aid preparation. Once you use them regularly and become more familiar with them, you will find it easier to know which may be more useful or important for a par-ticular dispute.

Contents of the toolkit:

1. BATNA and WATNA
2. Risk analysis
3. Potential outcome analysis
4. Plasticine
5. Decision analysis
6. Logistics and other points

Before looking at these, please do remember what Lewis Carroll's Alice said: 'I think I should understand that better, if I had it written down: but I can't quite follow it as you say it.'[2] So the very best thing you can do to help your clients is to ensure that the preparation is in writing.

Why? Firstly, the very fact of putting points in writing helps you and your client clarify options, strategies and tactics.

Secondly, when mediation is under way, you and your client can refer to your written preparation, knowing that you will not have forgotten key points.

Thirdly, by writing things down you protect yourself. Try as we might, we never take in everything we hear. Your client is likely to hear only what she wants to and her memory of discussions may differ from yours. Many of the complaints against lawyers in Scotland are about alleged poor communication. What a lawyer says and what the client actually hears can be poles apart. Written preparation mitigates potential misunderstandings, formal complaints from your client, or possible refusal to pay your fee note.

Some of the items in the toolkit may seem to overlap. That doesn't really matter. Use whichever idea or combination of ideas best suits the complexity of the issues your client is facing. In practice, I suggest you consider BATNA/WATNA first. The other tools can be used in whatever order suits you and your client.

Tip

Following each of the tools discussed, there is a heading 'Who does what?'. The allocations of responsibilities are intended solely as suggestions rather than as rules. There may be some things which it is obvious that you should prepare, and others that your client may be best-placed to do. It may not matter who does which parts, but what is essential is that you both know (in writing) who is responsible for what.

BATNA and WATNA

You may have already heard these terms being bandied around. The concept of BATNA (best alternative to a negotiated agreement) was developed by Fisher and Ury[3] in 1981 and is oft-quoted as a tool for negotiation. WATNA (worst alternative) evolved at a later stage. These terms are often discussed by academics and mediators as being part of the mediation itself. I don't particularly like that idea, as I find the concept difficult to explain readily during the meeting. In my view, anyone can negotiate a deal – it just depends on how much either party wants to receive or give away. It's still a deal if one party ends up paying a lot more for a product than it's really worth (as you'll know if you've ever haggled in a street market in Marrakech).

However, it would be remiss of me to exclude a mention of the Fisher and Ury tool.

The way I use the ideas behind BATNA and WATNA is in my early discussions with lawyers and/or potential clients. Generally I do not use the terms themselves. The question I ask is: 'If you aren't able to resolve this through mediation, what are the alternative options?'

Practical example

Let's assume that you have a great client, Liz, for whom you've done lots of different types of work over the years. She comes to you with a problem. Liz hired a car for a weekend from Dave, who runs a local outlet specialising in renting vintage cars. Unfortunately the car broke down, and when Liz called the office the staff were unhelpful and abrupt. Liz has taken umbrage at this and tells you the company shouldn't get away with such appalling service. She wants her hire charge back and some compensation.

You think mediation may be a useful way to resolve matters and have used the SPIN° approach to bring it to the attention of Liz. However, she remains unconvinced, so you move to the question 'If you aren't able to resolve this through mediation, what are the alternative options?'. Together you develop a list, which might include:

1. Bringing a court action to recover the cost of the hire and a claim for compensation for stress and inconvenience.
2. Writing a letter to the local newspaper complaining about the hire company.
3. Dropping leaflets through doors of local residents telling them how bad the company is.
4. Standing in front of the company's office with a sign saying how awful it is.
5. Telling all her friends on social media.
6. Doing a video about her experience and loading it onto YouTube.
7. Just forgetting the whole thing but never using the company again.

If mediation is not the preferred option, you and Liz discuss which alternative on the list would suit her best (BATNA), given what she wants to achieve, and how much time and energy she wants to put into this. You can then look at the WATNA (worst alternative). Is Liz really the sort of person who wants to stand in the rain all day waving a placard?

Liz decides initially that she wants to bring a court action. You are then able to talk through what is involved (your fees if you represent her, how much of her time it would take if she represents herself, likelihood of success, how if successful she would collect any monies, effect on her ability to rent a vintage car whenever she wants, etc.)

After hearing all this Liz may still decide to go to court. Fair enough: that's her call, and at least you've helped her make an informed decision by looking at alternatives. You've also discharged your obligations to assist her in decision-making.

(Of course, the audience who watched the YouTube clip of musician Dave Carroll singing to the world about how United Airlines broke his guitar may decide that their BATNA is to copy his approach to dispute resolution.)

Alternatively, Liz now feels that mediation may be the best option to try first. She knows that, if mediation doesn't result in an agreement, she can turn to her BATNA and go to court. Liz asks you to approach Dave's lawyer, and now it's their turn to do a BATNA/WATNA.

Their list may look like this:

1. Pay Liz what she wants to get rid of her.
2. Take her on at her own game and let everyone know how she always wants something extra for nothing.
3. Call the police if she stands outside the front of the office with a placard.
4. Threaten to take legal action against her if she distributes material adversely affecting your reputation.

Dave could decide that he would rather just pay her off and not waste any more time on this – his BATNA. Does Dave really want to go through hassle and potential bad PR by taking legal action against Liz if she tries to blacken his name (WATNA)?

Dave's lawyer discusses the potential outcomes of these alternatives with him. Now that Dave understands the various paths he could take, he opts for mediation. Hurray!

Who does what for BATNA/WATNA?

You

Ask: 'If you aren't able to resolve this through mediation, what are the alternative options?'
Think of some possible alternatives so that, if your client has difficulty getting off the mark, you can assist her.
Write down all the alternatives without initially assessing or criticising them.
Provide legal advice as appropriate about the alternatives, once the list is complete.
Start managing your client's expectations.

Client

Think of alternatives to settlement.
Take a decision about BATNA, either following or ignoring your advice.

Both

Discuss the alternatives.

Risk analysis

The next tool is risk analysis. In his article *Systematic Risk Analysis*, Professor John Wade takes a systematic approach to the structure of such an analysis, and in his conclusion says: 'The writer's hope is that the evolving written risk analysis will become a routine document in the offices of professional conflict managers – particularly lawyers and mediators.'[4] Not only will a written assessment of the priorities and risks help your client make more informed decisions, it can be a useful tool in managing her expectations.[5]

Let's look at another example of a dispute and use the risk analysis tool. Your client, Global IT Solutions, supplies software to Random, a large company with offices throughout the UK. Random alleges that your client has provided it with programs which do not meet the contractual specification and that it has suffered loss as a consequence. They are threatening court action, seeking €1,200,000 from your client. Global believes that the programs have been corrupted by changes made by Random's IT department. The parties have agreed to participate in mediation in an effort to resolve their differences. You are helping your client to prepare. You have advised the CEO of the legal aspects, but in your opinion she has not considered properly the effect this dispute may have if it is not resolved. You recommend that she analyses these effects.

There is no set format for a risk analysis, other than that it *must* be in writing (absolutely no point in doing it otherwise). The aim is to help your client assess the overall impact of this dispute on her business and, if relevant, on the people involved.

Example

Some of the impact may be financial.

1. What is the potential cost of our time spent on this if it is resolved at mediation?
   a. CEO   £
   b. Finance Director   £
   c. Software developer   £. . . . .
   d. Subtotal

2. What is the potential cost of our time spent on this if it is taken through court?

    a. CEO £

    b. Finance Director £

    c. Software developer £. . . . .

    d. Subtotal

3. Cost of expert witnesses £

4. Court costs £

5. Even if we successfully defend this action, how much of our costs will not be covered? £

6. What is the lost opportunity cost of this dispute? (In other words, what's the value of business opportunities we may miss while we are focusing on this dispute?) £

7. Cost of losing existing customers who find out that Random thinks we haven't delivered on the contract £

Some of the impact may be on people.

8. How will this affect morale within our company?

9. How will the stress of this dispute affect me/my family?

10. The FD hasn't been well for the past year. How might this affect his health?

Chances of success in court.

11. What are the percentages for each element of the dispute?

12. What are the odds of Random proving that point in court?

13. What are the odds of all or parts of any counter-claim succeeding?

14. What percentage chance do we have of proving that Random's IT department is responsible for the problems with the software?

Other considerations.

15. Random is a major customer of ours. If they refuse to work with us in the future, what impact will that have on our business?

16. How certain are we that a judge will understand the technical side of software development and believe our evidence?

17. How long will a court action take?

18. How might this dispute affect our reputation in the industry?

19. What negative PR may come out of a public dispute?

20. Most Important Question (see below).

Depending on the situation, it may be appropriate to have Global's entire management team undertake this analysis. This increases the likelihood of a more comprehensive assessment of the impact of the dispute on the business as a whole. It is best if the client, rather than the lawyer, completes the bulk of this analysis. The reason for this is that you are the expert on the legal side and your client is the expert on the business side. She has the knowledge to consider the questions and possible answers. As the lawyer you could provide an initial list of questions and then ask your client to add others if appropriate.

During this process, your client should also write down the risks from the other party's point of view and analyse these as best she can.

The use of the risk analysis tool is another way of reinforcing to your client that she is in control of what's discussed at mediation and of any outcome. It's her call to decide what issues are important to her and what risks she wants to bear.

Tip

The Most Important Question to add to the bottom of the risk analysis is along the following lines: 'When this dispute is over, what do you want things to look like?'

The reason for the question is that it focuses your client on where her real interests lie. The response might be: 'Random have spent a lot of time and money bringing this action. It doesn't matter whether I've won or lost. I just want them to suffer.' Or: 'The issues have been sorted out and we continue to do business with Random.'

Encouraging your client to consider the end point focuses her mind on the best way to get there.

Who does what for the risk analysis?

You

Prepare draft risk analysis sheet.
Explain the purpose to your client.
Encourage her to include other people in the risk analysis preparation if appropriate.
Provide advice about the likelihood of successfully proving relevant points in court.

> Advise amount of potential costs if the dispute is litigated.
>
> Help your client differentiate between her stated position and his real interests (by asking appropriate questions – see Chapter 7 for ideas).
>
> At the bottom of the risk analysis, write: 'When this dispute is over, what do you want things to look like?'

Client

> Complete the risk analysis as much as possible, adding any other relevant considerations.

Both

> Discuss and finalise the risk analysis.
>
> Discuss and use as part of strategy and tactics preparation.

Potential outcomes analysis

This is another part of your toolkit. You and your client consider possible solutions to the dispute and analyse the pros and cons of each.

Back to Liz and Dave and the problems resulting from the car hire. You and Liz have decided that there is no need for you to attend this mediation. However, Liz does ask for your help to work out how she can make the best deal at mediation. She says she wants a refund of the hire charges of £400, plus £200 compensation for all the hassle. Liz is fairly well-off, and although the money is important to her, you've discovered that she's a vintage car fanatic. She loves driving different cars and had been pleased to find Dave's outlet so handy for her workplace. Let's jump ahead and see what may have happened at mediation.

Potential outcome with limited or no preparation

The meeting progressed, but as neither Liz nor Dave had prepared properly, they found themselves coming to an agreement simply to end their feelings of discomfort.

By the end of the mediation, Liz and Dave have agreed that he will return the £400 for the hire charge and pay Liz £100 compensation. Both leave the meeting feeling relieved that the matter is over, but slightly dissatisfied with what they have got out of it. Liz had a fixed idea that her stress was worth £200, and she hasn't got that. She knows too that she can never go back to Dave's place to rent a car as it would be too awkward. Dave is peeved because he's lost the profit on the hire and had to pay extra on top of that when it wasn't his fault that the car broke down.

Potential outcome with good preparation

With proper preparation the agreement might have been different. In her preparation, Liz had considered potential outcomes. She'd thought the possibilities were:

1. Dave could return her £400 and give her some compensation.
2. Dave could return her money but refuse to give compensation.
3. Dave could offer her a free weekend car hire.
4. No agreement is reached.

At mediation, Dave offers to give Liz two weekends of car hire over the next 12 months at no charge, to resolve the issue. Was this a good deal for both?

From Liz's perspective, she had already considered the possibility of Dave giving her one weekend hire, so two seems a bonus. She also knew in advance that she wanted to have a few weekends away in the summer and the car hire would have been £400 a time. This deal was worth £800 (2 x £400) to her, so she feels she is getting an extra £200 as any court action would have been for only £600. She also feels that she's getting two weekend's hire 'free'. She's delighted. (Of course, the reality is that if she had been successful in court, she would still have been only £200 better off, as she'd already paid the £400 for the original car hire. With even better preparation she might have worked this out ahead of the mediation and made a different decision. Alternatively, she might have thought that, as she'd already spent the original £400, anything on top of that was a bonus.)

What about from Dave's point of view? He has prepared well and has thought through his potential outcomes.

Potential outcome one – pay Liz the £600 she's seeking and move on with life. However, being an astute businessman, Dave realises that simply doing this will not help his firm's reputation in the local area. He's been building the business up over the last couple of years and doesn't want Liz to start bad-mouthing him.

Potential outcome two – think of a solution which exceeds Liz's expectations so that she will tell her mates how he went the extra mile, thus enhancing his reputation. Dave has worked out a potential offer to make to Liz and how much it will cost him. He realises that he must make up his lost profit and calculates as follows.

Fixed cost for a weekend rental	£140
Profit on weekend rental	£260
Total	£400
2 weekends	£800
To recoup that he must make £800 in profit, so he needs to rent out an additional 3–4 cars (£800/£260)	

Dave knows, though, that his existing satisfied customers refer him to an average of two friends or colleagues each. He thinks Liz will now gain him two new customers who will then refer him to four more. Six additional cars hired out. Even if he only gets three referrals, he's decided that maintaining a good reputation is worth the difference, as advertising costs much more than that.

If, at mediation, Liz demanded four weekends' rental instead, Dave would already know whether that was something he could agree to or not. (To recoup £1,600 profit he would need to rent out an additional six or seven cars.) Liz has turned out to be a bit of a nightmare and he thinks she'll never be happy or recommend him, so he doesn't agree.)

Sidebar

You may be familiar with the expression 'expanding the pie', a term used in writings about finding creative solutions. The idea is that you don't limit yourself to the obvious – that you look beyond the scope of what's in front of you. That's the sort of thing you want to develop with your client. Here's a practical example based on a real situation.

In a coastal town in Australia there were two businesses which supplied filtered water in bottles, and in the large containers for use in offices. Between them they had the market covered, so if one tried to take a bit more market share by price-cutting, the other suffered and neither gained any long-term benefit. Both owners were becoming frustrated by the perceived lack of opportunity to expand their businesses. They consulted Bright Spark, a marketing guru.

Bright Spark realised that the only way for both the businesses to grow was to increase the number of people who drink filtered water. Being a highly-paid marketing consultant, he thought creatively: 'The town is beside the sea. At the sea there are seagulls. Seagulls sit on the roofs of houses, and do what seagulls do. When the rain comes, their poop is washed into the gutters of the houses. The gutters feed into the rainwater tanks which lots of Aussie homes have to collect fresh water in. People then drink this "fresh" water.'

Bright Spark came up with an advertising jingle which described all that, and the two businesses bought some airtime on local radio stations. Result – huge increase in bottled water consumption. Both businesses expanded without taking anything away from each other.

That's expanding the pie!

Who does what for potential outcome analysis?

You

Consider potential outcomes before discussing with your client.
Clarify in your own mind how you will explain financial calculations to her.
Prepare a pro forma or memory-jogger to help you and your client assess new options during private sessions at mediation (or for client to use if you do not attend mediation with her).

Both

Brainstorm potential outcomes, possibly using your initial thoughts as a starting point.
Work through financials together so your client understands her options.
Use pro forma as suggested above.

Plasticine

Obviously I don't mean the actual modelling clay. I use the term to illustrate that viable solutions can take on many different shapes. If your client locks herself into a single resolution (the clay in the shape of a cube for instance), she may miss the opportunity to benefit from a better solution which looks like a cylinder but still uses the same amount of clay. Let's look at an example using a familiar experience of buying a car.

Example

Your old banger is starting to cost you a lot for maintenance, so you've decided to trade it in for a two-year-old second-hand car. You've done your research online and found out that your car should be worth £2,000.

Potential outcome one – turn up at the car franchise and tell them you want £2,000 (this is your cube of clay) for yours or they don't have a deal. They may agree instantly. Know any dealers like that? Alternatively they may say 'thanks but no thanks' and you don't have the replacement car of your dreams. Your cube is completely flattened and you walk away with a manky bit of clay.

Potential outcome two – turn up at the car franchise knowing that your car is worth about £2,000 if someone is willing to pay you that. The dealer offers you £1,500 and free servicing for a year on your replacement car. Is this a good offer? (Is there the same amount of plasticine in this shape?)

Unless you have prepared, you may not know. If the car has to be serviced twice a year at £250 a time, then maybe it is. What if servicing is only needed once a year and costs only £150? What if? What if?

If you know that the servicing is worth £500 to you, then your cube is still the same volume but it looks like a rectangle. No problem. You accept the deal.

Potential outcome three – you ideally want £2,000 trade-in. However, if you can't get that you would settle for less, as long you don't have to worry about unexpected repairs (your BATNA). The dealer offers you £1,200 trade-in and a year's warranty for parts and service. It's not possible to put a monetary figure on this warranty as neither you nor the dealer know if problems will occur in the next 12 months. However, you've prepared. You know that peace of mind is important for you. You're not entirely sure if you'll end up with the same amount of plasticine, but now that it's rolled out into a cylinder it looks pretty comfortable and you accept the offer.

What about the £2,000? Of course, you could have waited until you found someone willing to give you that amount. It's not a certainty, but it is your call. At least you've made your decisions on the basis of good preparation and knowledge of what is important for you.

There is a much more academic explanation for this suggested tool. Leigh Thompson[6] prefers to call it the 'reservation point'. In her view, 'The reservation point is not determined by what the negotiator wishes and hopes for, but rather, by what her BATNA represents'.[7]

She provides an example involving selling a house, and gives a four-step process to determine a reservation price:

1. Brainstorm your alternatives
2. Evaluate each alternative
3. Attempt to improve your BATNA
4. Determine your reservation price[8]

If you are interested in learning more about negotiation, I recommend that you read this book.

Example

This time you are acting for a family owned business (FOB) which employs 300 people and has a turnover of €27 million. They are selling the business and ideally want €3 million for it. FOB had entered into a contract with International Conglomeration (IC), who are now disputing the turnover figures and want to reduce their offer or withdraw from the deal. FOB admits to you that there can be different interpretations of the turnover figures. You work with FOB to determine their reservation point.

FOB say that they have a 40 per cent chance of getting the €3 million they are seeking from another buyer. They also feel that if they reduced the price to €2.75 million, the chance of a sale in the next year would go up to 85 per cent. (Of course, this has to be reduced to 45 per cent to take into account the 40 per cent chance already considered.) FOB estimate that there's a 15 per cent chance of no sale in the next year. So the maths are:

€3,000,000 x 40%	=	€1,200,000
plus		
€2,750,000 x 45%	=	€1,237,500
plus		
zero x 15%	=	€0
Reservation point	=	€2,437,500

Once you and FOB know this (and you've undertaken a risk assessment), your client can then decide whether to accept a lower offer from IC or threaten to instigate legal proceedings to enforce the contract.

I realise that this example does not take into account all factors – for instance, the NPV (Net Present Value of money) or the intangibles such as stress on the family. What you are doing here is helping your client to consider the situation from another perspective (moulding the clay differently) and to build a better base of information from which to make an informed decision. She may decide that insisting on €3 million is not necessarily the best option for her.

Who does what with the plasticine?

You

Explain the idea to your client.
Demonstrate how to work it out.

Client

Provide information: for example, cost of servicing, likelihood of a sale of her business at full price/reduced price.

Both

Work out what the BATNA represents and use it as part of strategic/ tactical planning.

Decision analysis

This is a process to help you and your client analyse percentage chances and subsequent financial impacts. For instance, you might assess that, for a £10 bet on the races, you have a one in seven chance of winning £2,000. Alternatively you could invest your tenner in a charity raffle and have a one in ten chance of winning theatre tickets worth £40. You map out the decision point, estimate the percentages and look at the possible financial outcomes (Figure 6.1).

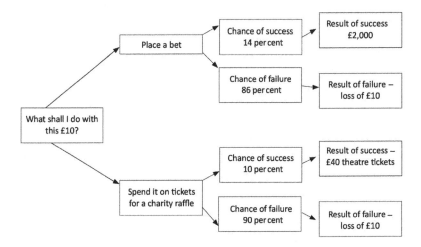

Figure 6.1   Decision analysis 1

So now you have analysed the percentage chances and the financial impacts of your decision about where to invest your £10. The results of success are markedly different, while the results of failure are the same.

Remember, though, the Most Important Question mentioned in the section about risk analysis: 'When this dispute is over, what do you want things look like?' Substitute the question 'After you've invested your £10, what do you want things to look like?'. If your answer is 'I want to have won £2,000' then the decision may be to put a stake on the next race although the chance of winning £2,000 is low. Your decision may be different if you reply 'It'd be great to win the theatre tickets, but if I don't, at least my £10 will go to a good cause'.

The purpose of this analysis tool is to weigh up the financial impact of decisions and assess how they support or detract from what's important to your client after the dispute is resolved. It is another useful process to help ensure that your client has the best possible basis on which to make an *informed* decision. And yes, it is used by lawyers. As Arron and Hoffer note:

> Long used by business people to model business decisions, decision analysis has more recently gained recognition within the legal community as a tool for decision making in complex litigation.[9]

Let's go back to your client involved in the software dispute, Global IT.

Given that the CEO of Global IT now has a better understanding of the risks of not resolving the dispute at all, she can turn to a consideration of the stages at which she may have to make interim decisions. As her adviser, you guide her through this process.

In the analysis of potential outcomes, one you've both thought about is that Random may reduce its demands to, say, £100,000 because they may just want to sort matters quickly. How does this stack up against your assessment of success in a court action? (Let's assume that the BATNA is to defend the action in court. Global wants to be able to work out if the suggestion is better than the BATNA.)

You think that Global is in a fairly strong position to defend any court action and estimate a 60 per cent chance of success. However, there are decisions to be made (Figure 6.2).

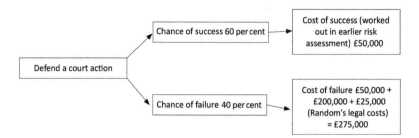

Figure 6.2   Decision analysis 2

Your client may feel that paying £100,000 is better than the risk of possibly paying £275,000 for failure. Alternatively she may feel that if she's going to pay £100,000 when she has a 60 per cent chance of winning, she wants to add something to the pot so that she increases her chances of retaining Global as a customer. Again, you've both prepared and you know that Global's business is worth £80,000 a year to Random. The discussions may then take the path of agreeing to fix the current problems and pay the £100,000 under certain conditions. For example, Random will extend their contract with your client for three more years and add in the work for their new premises, which open in six months' time.

Obviously this example is not an exact science – and in real life, your client's position won't be either. What is essential is that you have looked at the numbers, considered the odds, assessed the possibilities and put your client in the best possible position to make decisions during the mediation itself.

Who does what in a decision analysis?

You

Prepare flow chart of potential decision points before meeting with client.

Both

Consider options which arose during the potential outcomes analysis.
Discuss and adapt initial flow chart before the mediation.
In private sessions during mediation, use flow chart as a working tool to aid consideration of options.

Logistics and other points

In addition to the written preparation, you should take responsibility for a number of practical matters:

1. Information for the mediator
    Ask the mediator what information she needs to read before the mediation. This will vary, depending on the complexity of the issues and/or the mediator's preferences. Personally I don't ask for a lot of background detail because as mediator I am not there to make a decision. What I find useful is a short summary (perhaps a couple of pages) of the key issues for your client, or a copy of the Closed Record, or the Claim, or Defence. Other mediators may ask for more detail.

2. Documents at the ready
    Ensure that you (or your client) have all relevant background and/or supporting documents for the mediation. Have copies available for the other party and mediator if you think these will help the discussion.
    Some lawyers and/or parties are concerned about producing documents at mediation which the other party might use against them. Remember that mediation is not an adversarial process. The idea is to try to find a solution which suits all. If a particular document can help towards this, then I suggest you include it in the spirit of the process.

3. 'Right' people at the table
    Ensure that the 'right' people attend the mediation. As you can see in the example of the Agreement to Mediate in Appendix 5, the parties confirm that they have 'authority to settle'. If your client is a business or is representing other family members, for example, she *must* have authority to make decisions which bind the company or others. It's a waste of everyone's time (and money) if fruitful discussions have taken place, terms of an agreement sorted, and then one party turns around and says 'Of course, I'll have to get my Board's approval for this first'.
    If such approval is going to be necessary, encourage your client to obtain it in advance or make it quite clear to the other party and the mediator, before the mediation takes place, that matters can only be taken so far.

The 'right' people may also include other advisers such as an accountant, a technical expert, or a representative of an insurance company. It may be the person who actually did the work which is the subject of the dispute or complaint. For further points about 'extras', see Appendix 15.

4. Client expectations

There's not a lot of point in allowing your client to go in to mediation with unrealistic expectations. You can help her and the process greatly by reminding her that the other party is likely to have a different point of view; that mediation may not end in an agreement; that simply because she wants £50,000 compensation doesn't mean she's going to receive it, etc. etc. The old adage 'Under-promise and over-deliver' is good to keep in mind.

5. Client coaching

There may be some points which your client feels uncertain or uncomfortable about making during mediation. You can help her practise these in advance, trying out different ways to make it easier for her.

For example, it could be that your client's style is to go in with all guns blazing. You may feel that this would be counter-productive. As her adviser you may find it prudent to point this out to her and suggest a different form of words.

Likewise, if your client is worried about how she will cope if the other party loses his temper or starts crying, talk about it beforehand and help her develop coping mechanisms.

Sidebar

When I'm talking with a party in private session, I will often ask him to try out what he plans to say to the other when we're all back in the same room. Attempt one might be: 'I still think that I'm right, but to get rid of this mess I'll give you £200.' I would then ask him how he thinks the other person might react to that approach, or how he would feel if those words were spoken to him. Attempt two (three or four) might end up as: 'We do have different points of view about who's right and who's wrong. However, I'd like to resolve this so we can both move on. I'm prepared to give you £200 if you agree to draw a line under this dispute.

6. Stamina

For a long mediation, everyone needs lots of stamina. Tell your client that it may be a tiring day so that she can prepare for that. You need to be on the ball too. Try to get a good sleep the night before and avoid having to deal with other clients' calls or your office staff during the mediation.

And one more thing . . .

At the beginning of the mediation, the mediator will invite each party to make a brief opening statement. She sets the scene by saying something like: 'This is an opportunity for you to tell each other how you see the dispute from your point of view. It's also a chance for you to really listen to each other. If it's OK with you, I'd like each of you to talk briefly [she may indicate a rough time limit] and for the other person not to interrupt. So for example, when Liz is talking, Dave, it would be good if you don't interrupt. Then it will be your turn, and, Liz, I'd ask that you don't interrupt. Do you agree to this?'

This is the one part of the mediation which you know will definitely happen and you know when that will be. Thus your client can prepare what she wants to say.

The opening statement should be succinct and non-inflammatory. It should state the facts and the impact of the alleged fault, breach of contract, poor service, etc. For example, Liz might say: 'Thank you for agreeing to come to mediation, Dave. As you know, I hired a car for a weekend from you, but unfortunately it broke down. When I called your office the person I spoke to seemed very unhelpful and I felt she was rather abrupt with me. I was upset that the car had broken down because I'd been planning to spend the weekend in the country. Then on top of that I felt annoyed that I'd been treated so badly by your staff. From my point of view, I think the service was poor and I don't think that's the way you should treat your customers. I would like you to refund the hire charge and also give me some compensation for all the upset.'

If only all opening statements were like that. In reality, of course, a party who hasn't prepared often goes into all the minutiae of what went wrong, assigns blame completely to the other person, and starts to lock herself into a fixed position. It takes an experienced mediator to strike the right balance between letting someone vent their feelings and allowing her to accuse or dominate before the other party has had a chance to speak.

When a party thanks the other for agreeing to mediate, she acknowledges the voluntary nature of mediation. She recognises that the other party has made a financial and time commitment to try to sort out matters between them. In my experience, an expression of thanks helps set a positive tone for the meeting. Another helpful approach to take (if it is appropriate) is to encourage your client to start by making an apology – especially if she is the one who is allegedly in the wrong. (See Chapter 7 for some suggested words.) As Associate Professor Prue Vines writes,

> where a proper apology is made it can operate as a form of redress which equalises (at least to some extent) the relationship between the parties.[10]

In the Liz and Dave situation, which is based loosely on a real mediation at a Sheriff Court, Dave's first words were along the lines of 'I'm sorry that things seem to have gone wrong for you and that you felt you had to bring the court action'. That rather took the wind out of Liz's sails and set the tone for a fruitful discussion.

Who does what for the opening statement?

You

Tell your client that the mediator will ask each party to make an opening statement.
Guide your client with the content.
Advise your client that it is her statement, so she should feel comfortable with what she is saying and how she is saying it.
Don't offer to make the opening statement (remind your client that it's her meeting).

Client

Uses her own words.
Ideally writes them down or at least has bullet points to refer to.
Uses non-inflammatory language.
Sets the tone – conciliatory if possible.
Recognises different points of view.

Both

Decide who will make the opening statement (ideally, the client).
Consider tactics, for example how to present a united front (see below under *Opening*).

Sidebar

I have heard mediation referred to as 'just a facilitated negotiation'. Yes and no. If all that is being discussed is money, then the meeting should be called 'a negotiation involving a third party'. If there is more to it – clarifying understanding, recognising interests, continuing relationships, improving communication – then to me this becomes more than negotiation.

Of course, once the intangibles are dealt with, it may be that part of the resolution comes down to money. Before entering into mediation, this may be the most important thing for your client. She may look to you for advice about what sort of deal she should hold out for.

But there is no fixed answer. Instead your role is to help her prepare by using the contents of the toolkit so she can make her own informed decision. She can then walk away from the mediation knowing that whatever the outcome, she has made the best possible decision in the circumstances.

During mediation

It will not always be necessary to attend the mediation with your client. The decision is usually based on the complexity of the dispute and/or the level of confidence of the client and should be discussed at the preparation stage. If you are present at the mediation, you are there to support your client, the mediator and the process. Over the years I have found that the lawyers who are most effective at mediation are those who are patient, flexible and realistic. (For insights from another mediator, you may care to read the article by Greg Vickery.[11])

Opening

During the preparation stage, you and your client will have agreed who should make the opening statement. If she has insisted that you do this, it is best to avoid becoming Rumpole. Remember that mediation is about working towards a mutually acceptable solution. This is not the place for displaying your adversarial skills, or for quoting chapter and verse of the relevant legislation or case law.

If your client chooses to speak for herself, then I suggest you resist the temptation to jump in at this early stage to add more points or to elaborate in any way. There will be plenty of time for clarification later. If you intervene unnecessarily, it can quickly change the non-adversarial tone of the meeting which the mediator would have tried to establish at the start. You could also irritate your client, who thinks 'Hang on. We'd agreed I was going to talk during this bit. Why is he jumping in already? He told me this was a meeting between Fred and me and that he would just be here to support, not take over.' Think about your own experience of having a colleague, parent or partner interrupt your presentation (or your best joke) when you were just about to cover that point anyhow. It's annoying.

However, you may want to use tactics discussed in the section about preparation. For example, if you've decided that it's important to demonstrate a united front between you and your client, the following might happen – client makes the opening statement; at the end, she turns to you and asks if there is anything else; your response is always, 'No. I think that sums up how we see the situation.'

During the opening statement of the other party, you support your client by taking notes about the key points. This is far more than simply writing down what's being said. If you've prepared well you may have anticipated some of the points. Others may surprise you. Listen intently, not only to what the other party is saying, but to *how* he is saying it.

Tip

You may find it easier to have a page already drawn up with headings, like the following.

Agreed points	Disagree	Other's viewpoint	Thought starters
Equipment has broken down			
	Reason why it broke down	Faulty installation by my client. Irrational anger (why?)	How to check this? Has something else happened to make him so angry?

Your client is unlikely to be in the right state of mind to capture this information. As she hears the other party talking, she is probably either assessing how her own opening statement went, or rehearsing for her turn.

Under way

During joint sessions, the most effective lawyers always remember that it is the *parties'* meeting, not their own. Remember one of the key principles of mediation – the parties retain control of the outcome. You will have talked about this with your client when considering the mediation option with her. The mediator will have emphasised this too. Your role is to help the process and support your client. You are not there to argue fine points of law on behalf of your client, to dominate the discussion or to build up unnecessary barriers on the path to a settlement.

As was mentioned in Chapter 3, the meeting may move between joint and private sessions. If you feel at any stage that it would be helpful for you and your client to talk in a separate room, you should suggest that to her. This situation may arise if, for example, the other party has revealed new information which changes things for your client. It could be that some options are on the table and you want to discuss these with her. You may see that your client is becoming stressed or tearful and you consider it appropriate to have some breathing space. Such separate meetings may or may not include the mediator.

In private session, you and your client have the opportunity to discuss how things have progressed and to weigh up any options. You can play devil's advocate to remind your client of the interests she revealed to you during the preparation phase. This is also the time to provide any legal advice relating to options being considered. Be realistic about the chances of success through litigation. As an experienced mediator and ADR consultant writes,

> it really is not helpful to constantly repeat words to the effect that 'we are certain we are going to win'. This is not reality. Be constructive about acknowledging realistic litigation risks in private session with the mediator.[12]

Example

You are in a private session with your client and the mediator. You'd suggested the move because you could see your client was fuming at the other party's accusations.

Client	Do you hear what he said? He's blaming me completely for the breakdown. I know I installed the equipment properly. It's his maintenance people who don't know what they're doing. I told them to turn the machine off before rotating the widget wheel. I bet they didn't do that, so they're saying it's my fault. I've had enough. Let them take me to court and I'll show them how incompetent their staff are.
You	So, as we'd discussed last week in the office, your point of view is that you installed the machine properly and it's the maintenance which has caused the breakdown. The others have a different take on the situation, as we expected they would. I'm interested that you are thinking about court again. Remember you told me that you would like to keep Fred as a customer. How would going to court help you achieve that?
Client	You're right, it won't help, but I'm just so angry that they think I'm the only one to blame here.
You	There's nothing wrong with feeling angry, but let's look at our plan again and see the best way to clear the air and keep Fred's business.

Using your plans

We've looked at the importance of good preparation, and you will recall my emphasis on the need to have your plans in writing. The next thing to recognise is that these plans should not be rigid. They are there to guide you and help you evaluate progress and options during the discussion. Mediation can be an intense process. You need to keep your wits about you and maintain your concentration throughout. A written plan provides reference points and allows you to see where concessions may be acceptable to help your client satisfy her underlying interests.

In the simplified diagram below (Figure 6.3), your client wants to keep Fred as a customer. That's the goal. There are different ways to reach it.

In addition, the written plan provides you and your client with the map of where she'd like to end up (Figure 6.4).

If, during the mediation, your client decides on a different destination, then at least you will both know that it is a *chosen* end point, rather than one reached by succumbing to the other party.

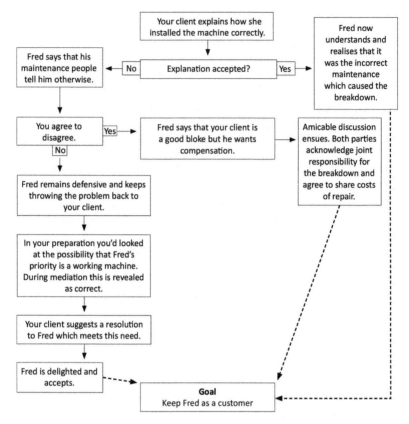

Figure 6.3   Methods of reaching the goal

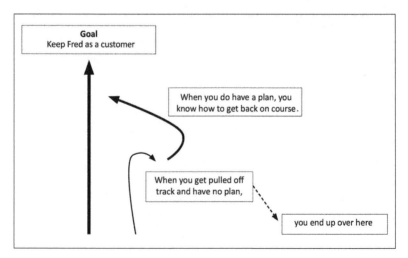

Figure 6.4   Map towards goal

Resolution

The mediation has progressed and a resolution has been reached. If the agreement is fairly straightforward, the terms may be written up there and then. (I refer to this as the Settlement Agreement.) The actual writing may well be done by the mediator, but the terms will be those of the parties as described in the example in Chapter 3 ('Jack, you said that you are willing to re-paint Tim's front door. When would you be able to do that by?'). This is where you again support your client by ensuring that the terms cover the points agreed.

In my experience, it is *not* essential to cover all the possibilities if something goes wrong. The reason is that by this stage the parties have reached a point where the issues have been thrashed about and a resolution has been reached, and each is in a frame of mind to fulfil his or her part of any agreement. There is generally a positive atmosphere in the room. If you then start suggesting terms along the lines of 'If Jack doesn't do what he says he will, then we'll see you in court' (a bit extreme, I know, but you get the gist), then the whole consensus may well fall apart. If you are concerned that a party may not complete his or her part of the bargain, then ensure that deadlines are inserted. So if Jack hasn't painted the front door by the agreed date, both parties know the deal has been broken and each can take whatever steps they wish to resolve matters.

Of course, if part of the Settlement Agreement relies on an absent third party doing something, it is best to build in contingencies in case it doesn't happen or there are delays. For example, Fred agrees to order and pay for the damaged part for the equipment. This has to come from a third-party supplier. The agreement may say something like:

> Fred agrees to order the part by 31 March. Once it has arrived, he will call [your client] within 48 hours to let her know. [Your client] will then repair the machine within seven working days.

Or:

> Fred agrees to order the part by 31 March. If the supplier is unable to provide the part, Fred will notify [your client] immediately. [Your client] will then advise Fred of the cost of a new machine within seven working days.

If the resolution is more complex, it may be that you and the other party's lawyer need to take some time after the meeting to draw up agreed terms. In these circumstances, the mediator should ensure that the relevant points are recorded in writing as a 'Memorandum of Understanding', 'Interim Settlement Agreement' or other similarly-termed document. Everyone should leave the meeting absolutely clear about what's been agreed. The only thing remaining is for the lawyers to wrap the 'right' words around it.

Tip

Remember:

1. The *terms* of the Settlement Agreement are the parties', not the mediator's or the lawyers'; the *words* can be suggested by the parties, the mediator or the lawyers.
2. Once signed, the Agreement is a contract between the parties.
3. Critical points to cover are to record *exactly*:
   a. what action will be taken, by when, by whom – for example, 'A will pay B £20,000 by cheque by 30 August 2017'.
   b. what will happen to the dispute or any pending court action once the action is completed – for example, 'On receipt of cleared funds, B will draw up a Joint Minute to dismiss the action and will lodge it with the Court within 14 days of A signing the Joint Minute'.
4. Alternatively, the parties could agree basic terms and that the lawyers will draw up a formal document later. In such an instance, it is essential that the parties sign an interim agreement before they leave the mediation room. For example:

   The parties agree that their lawyers will, within 14 days of today's date, draft a Settlement Agreement which reflects the following:

   a. the parties' intention to void the commercial contract between them
   b. B to pay A £50,000 by 30 September 2017
   c. A to return the equipment by 1 October 2017
   d. The parties' agreement to sign this Settlement Agreement within 21 days of today's date
5. If you as a lawyer are drafting the Agreement, remember that it should reflect the terms and *intentions* agreed between the parties. Keep it simple. You don't want such a complex document that the parties end up in another dispute over what the terms meant.

Rant

Some mediators may suggest that it is best that absolutely everything is final-
ised before anyone leaves the meeting – even if this means working until the
small hours. I totally disagree with this approach. Mediation can be a tiring
experience. You may be in one room all day focusing on discussion, differing points of view, possible alternative solutions, emotions – it's exhausting
sometimes. The last thing you want is for your client to be 'forced' to finalise a Settlement Agreement and for you to have to craft the terms when your
brain is addled. The mediator may point out the difficulties of getting everyone together again or how it's important to finalise everything now while it's
current – but *resist*! You will do no favours to yourself or your client if you
end up with an agreement which lets you get to bed, but which you both
later regret. As a mediator, if I anticipate that a mediation may be lengthy and
difficult to finalise in a day, I suggest to clients that we schedule the extra time
in advance. If it's not needed, then there's no problem. Better that than parties
feeling squeezed into submission.

No resolution

As mentioned earlier, there is no guarantee that mediation will end
in complete agreement. However, there may still be a 'satisfactory'
outcome. If the dispute is complex, it may be that the issues have been
narrowed. Some may have been resolved to everyone's satisfaction,
while others remain for a court to decide. Even if there is no agreement, at least your client knows where she stands and can make
decisions about the way forward.

The most important thing is that you have managed your client's
expectations. Point out in advance, for example, 'If you can't resolve
matters at mediation, at least you will know that you've tried that
option. If you then decide to go to court, you will know that you are
choosing it as last resort.'

Sidebar

Even if a dispute isn't resolved during the mediation, it is often sorted fairly
soon afterwards. Once parties have had time to reflect on the discussions and
consider their WATNA, they may decide to reach a mutually acceptable solution. As mediator, I always leave the way open for parties to contact me with
an offer to pass on if they wish. Alternatively, I encourage the parties to talk
to each other if they later decide to reach an agreement to end their dispute.

Assessing the mediator

While the mediation is happening, you should take the opportunity to assess the mediator. Obviously this is not your top priority, but if you can get into the habit of doing so, you will find it helpful when you are reflecting on the process afterwards (as discussed below). To understand what to look for I suggest you read Appendix 9, 'Assessing mediator performance'. There you will see the reasoning behind the description of the flow of the mediation between Tim and Jack in Chapter 3. Also in the Appendices is a suggested checklist for assessing mediator performance. This includes points to look for during the mediation.

Post-mediation

Your role as a lawyer should not stop once the mediation is complete. Obviously, if steps have to be taken to complete all the terms of the Settlement Agreement, you will need to ensure that these occur.

Even if the end of the mediation means the end of the dispute, it is critical to reflect (and write down) what you did well, what you would do differently next time, and any other learning points. The point of this is that no two disputes or mediations are going to be exactly the same. By building up your understanding of the good/not so good experiences, you will be in a strong position to assist clients in future mediations. For a suggested pro forma, see Appendix 11, 'Assessing your own performance'.

In addition to looking at your own performance, it is important to assess that of the mediator. If you've done some of this already during the mediation, well and good. Do take the time, though, to look at the checklist[13] again after the mediation is finished. This reflection gives you the opportunity to record the mediator's style, her professionalism, and her strengths and weakness. When you are choosing a mediator for another client you can refer to this to see whether you feel this person's style would be appropriate for your client.

You may also consider it beneficial to your relationship with your client to confirm how this mediation has helped her. You have nothing to lose by reminding your client of your role. 'I am glad that my suggestion to try mediation has proved worthwhile.' Or, 'I am pleased that I was able to support you during the mediation and to help you achieve a satisfactory outcome.'

Of course, if mediation hasn't resulted in an agreement, it is just as important to keep in contact with your client. (Interestingly, more than 90 per cent of party litigants who responded to surveys carried out at Edinburgh Sheriff Court between 2004 and 2007 would recommend mediation to friends. An equally high percentage would use mediation again. Even if the dispute was not resolved at mediation, the responses to these questions remained positive.[14]) Sometimes solicitors feel embarrassed that things haven't worked out. If you've helped your client prepare properly, taken care when choosing the mediator and done your bit to provide support, the lack of a Settlement Agreement is not your fault.

As mediator, I sometimes agonise after an 'unsuccessful' mediation. Should I have done more? Could I have done something differently which would have resulted in agreement? Then I mentally kick myself. I did the best I possibly could at the time, and at the end of the day it is up to the parties whether or not they reach agreement. I go through all the positive parts – the fact that the parties were able to sit together in a room all day to discuss their difference; the fact that there was no blood on the floor. I then may think 'Perhaps in the future I could pay more attention to . . .' You may find a similar approach helpful.

Sidebar

I have not been able to find any official research into the rate of compliance with Settlement Agreements reached at mediation. In my own experience and that of colleagues, it is extremely rare (less than 1 per cent) for parties not to fulfil the terms agreed. This makes perfect sense when you think about the mediation process:

1. The parties participate voluntarily.
2. Before they start, they sign an agreement which says 'Each Party will attempt in good faith to resolve the dispute using the mediation process and will attend the mediation with full authority to settle the dispute'.[15]
3. They control the outcome.
4. They don't have to agree to anything they don't want to.
5. They can shape the terms in whatever way they wish.

Given all that, it is not surprising that the parties honour the commitments they've made.

Summary

- Use the contents of your toolkit to prepare both yourself and your client.
- Always put preparation in writing.
- Ask 'When this dispute is over, what do you want things to look like?'
- Write down who's doing what.
- Think of creative solutions.
- Support your client, the mediator and the process.
- Use checklists to ensure nothing is forgotten. (See suggested checklists in the Appendices.)
- Always follow up with your client.
- Assess the mediator during (if possible) and after.
- Reflect on what worked well and what might work better next time.

Notes

1. Trevor, 'The more things change'.
2. Carroll, *Alice in Wonderland*.
3. Fisher and Ury, *Getting to Yes*, Chapter 6.
4. Wade, *Systematic Risk Analysis*.
5. Remember the point about clients' perception of 'success' depending largely on how their expectations are managed.
6. Thompson, *The Mind and Heart of the Negotiator*.
7. Ibid., p. 17.
8. Ibid., pp. 17–19.
9. Aaron and Hoffer, 'Decision analysis', p. 363.
10. Vines, 'Apologies and civil liability'.
11. Vickery, 'Seven principles'.
12. Middleton-Smith, 'Mediation advocacy'.
13. Appendix 9.
14. Collation of figures from reports of the Edinburgh Sheriff Court Mediation Service from September 2004 to August 2007, written by the author.
15. Agreement to Mediate.

Chapter 7

MIX 'N' MATCH

When you're talking about work issues that you deal with every day, it's easy for the right words, phrases and sentences to roll off your tongue. Until you become more familiar with mediation, the following may help you in discussions with clients. (Rather than continuing to refer to 'the other party', I've decided to call him Max.)

For you

What's mediation about?

1. 'Mediation gives you the chance to sit down with Max and see if you can sort things out with the help of the mediator.'
2. 'With mediation you have the opportunity to let Max know how all this has affected you.'
3. 'If you want to go to court that's fine. However, once that happens, the result is out of your control. With mediation, you and Max decide the outcome.'
4. 'If you don't want to run the risk of your competitors finding out about this dispute mediation is ideal, because you can discuss matters with Max confidentially at mediation.'
5. 'Mediation is voluntary, so I certainly won't twist your arm. It would be a waste of your money if you went to the meeting unwillingly. However, it's a good opportunity for you and Max to sit down with an independent person to see if you can sort things out.'

What are the pros and cons of mediation?

1. 'Mediation is generally much faster than other processes. With a dispute such as this, it would probably last no longer than a day.'
2. 'One good thing about mediation is that it doesn't drag on forever. If you decide to go through more formal routes, it could take months or years before everything is sorted out.'

3. 'Usually a mediation can be arranged fairly quickly. If Max agrees as well, then it would just be a matter of sorting out a date which suits everyone.'
4. 'With mediation you know in advance how much it will cost.'
5. 'While the law might be on your side, it could be an expensive option to litigate.'
6. 'It's much easier to keep costs under control with mediation than it is with litigation.'
7. 'With mediation, you and Max control the outcome so you won't have to have anything imposed on you.'
8. 'You and Max can work out your own solutions at mediation. You'll have the breathing space to look at possible outcomes so you won't have to make concessions you don't want to.'
9. 'Because mediation is confidential, no one else will find out details about your business.'
10. 'Mediation is confidential so you and Max can talk openly about what's gone wrong.'
11. 'A downside of mediation is that there is no guarantee that you and Max will reach an agreement. However, the odds are pretty good, so let's have a look at the pros and cons.'
12. 'If you and Max reach an agreement, there is the possibility that he may not go through with his part of the deal. However, from what I understand about mediation, this is really unusual. It seems that when parties have worked out things together, they are much more likely to honour the agreement.'

How does mediation work?

1. 'Usually there are at least two rooms available for the meeting. The mediator will probably meet with you and Max together in one room first. This is when you'll get an opportunity to tell Max your point of view and for you to listen to his. Then you might all stay together or you could meet privately with the mediator in the other room. It's flexible, so sometimes you might all be together and other times in different rooms. The idea is to see if you and Max can work out an agreement that you can both live with.'
2. 'You don't have to talk about things you don't want to.'
3. 'You won't have to agree to anything you don't want to.'
4. 'The mediator doesn't take sides. She's there to help you and Max have a worthwhile discussion with the aim of sorting things out.'

5. 'If you and Max reach agreement, then we'll write up the terms there and then for you both to sign. Alternatively, you could reach some form of interim understanding, then Max's lawyer and I would draft a Settlement Agreement later.'

Managing expectations

1. 'There's no guarantee that you'll be able to resolve matters at mediation. But then there's no guarantee with other options either, I'm afraid.'
2. 'It may be that to sort things out with Max, you decide to give him some of the family's paintings he's asking for.'
3. 'It may be that not all the issues will be sorted at mediation. At least, though, you might be able to resolve some of them.'
4. 'During the mediation, you might feel that you're not going to be able to sort things out with Max. That's pretty normal. The mediator will work with you both to help move past that stage.'
5. 'If there's no agreement at mediation and you then decide to go to court, you will know that you are choosing it as last resort.'

Handling objections

1. Client: 'I'm right, he's wrong, so why should I mediate?'
   'From your point of view, you're right. Max seems to think differently. By sitting down together you'll have the chance to explain to him why you think you are right.'
2. Client: 'He's broken the contract – that's all there is to it.'
   'Even if that's the case, mediation gives you both the chance to sort out what will happen next. Remember that once this goes to court, the outcome is out of your control.'
3. Client: 'I'm not backing down from this. It's a point of principle.'
   'By mediating you are really bringing this to Max's attention. You can explain to him how important your principles are to you.'
4. Client: 'I can't stand to be in the same room with him so mediation will never work.'
   a. 'You don't necessarily have to be in the same room. Of course, mediation works a lot better if you at least start together, but let's talk to the mediator about that.'
   b. 'Fair enough. Would you be willing to give it a try if you start off in separate rooms?'

5. Client: 'If we go to mediation, Max will know all the points which we might want to bring up in court.'
   a. 'You're right. Remember, though, that discussions at mediation are confidential. If we ended up in court and Max tried to bring up things he only knew because of mediation, we would object, because of the confidentiality he's agreed to. The same would apply to us, of course.'
   b. 'You're right. He does already know most of our points, though, because of all the correspondence we've exchanged.'

6. Client: 'I don't know about this. Max is so unreasonable. What if he just won't listen during the mediation?'
   a. 'The mediator is experienced in dealing with all sorts of people. She will do her best to encourage him to take on board what you're saying.'
   b. 'That is something for you to think about. You know him better than I do. However, if he agrees to come to mediation, perhaps that's a sign that he is prepared to listen.'
   c. 'What makes you think Max is unreasonable?'
   d. 'That is a possibility. However, from my experience/ what the mediator tells me, most people who attend mediation voluntarily do want to find out how to sort things out.'

7. Client: 'Isn't this just going to be a negotiation and I'll have to compromise?'
   a. 'It's really more than just a negotiation. There may well be areas where both you and Max can agree something which will help you both. For example, in a recent mediation the parties realised they could both benefit by changing the way one was delivering goods to the other.'
   b. 'There may be some compromise involved, but remember you don't have to agree to anything you don't want to.'

8. Client: 'Max will certainly want his lawyer to come to the mediation with him. You know that I can't afford for you to come with me. They're bound to try to bully me into submission.'
   a. 'It sounds as though you feel Max might pressure you into something you don't want. Remember that because mediation is voluntary you could always tell Max that you'll mediate with him, but not if his lawyer is there.'

   b. 'It sounds as though you are worried that you'll agree to things you don't want to. Remember you have control over the outcome so you shouldn't be forced into anything. I'll show you (or I'll help you) prepare so that you'll feel confident in any decisions you make during the mediation.'

   c. 'It sounds as though you think you may not get a chance to put your point of view across. Remember that part of the mediator's role is to make sure that no one feels forced into agreements.'

Discovering the real interests of your client

   1. 'You've said that it's a point of principle for you that Max pays you. Could you explain that a little more for me please?'

   a. Client replies and you say 'So you want Max to know that he can't treat people like he's treated you. How would you have liked to have been treated?'

   b. Client replies and you say 'So it's important to you that people treat you respectfully'.

   2. 'You've said that the neighbour's birds are a menace. Could you clarify what you mean by "menace"?'

   a. 'So they have these blood-curdling screams which go on all day. How does that affect you?'

   b. 'So you aren't able to concentrate because of the noise. What's the impact of not being able to concentrate?'

   c. 'So not being able to concentrate affects your peace of mind and this means you are having difficulty completing your next film script. From what I hear you say, I understand it's important that you finish the script in the next two months.'[1]

   3. 'You have said that it's the airline's fault that you were stranded in Barcelona. Could you clarify for me how being stranded affected you?'

   a. 'You've said that the ash cloud from the volcano wasn't their fault so could you tell me how the airline could have helped you in a better way?'

   b. 'So, from what you say, I understand that you found it frustrating when they didn't tell you what was happening.'

   c. 'Am I right in thinking that it's important to you to be told what's going on?'

4. 'When Max installed the gate so you couldn't park close to your house, it caused problems for you. Could you tell me what sort of difficulties it's created?'
   a. 'So you need to be close to the house, so you can walk to the door quickly. Could you tell me why it's important to you to be able to get inside quickly?'
   b. 'If I have understood you correctly, you feel uncomfortable outside when you're alone so you're more relaxed once you're inside the house.'

What happens afterwards?

1. 'If the mediation settles, I'll follow up to make sure that you and Max each do what you've agreed. Once you've each done your bit, your dispute is at an end. You can then draw a line under this whole thing.'
2. 'If you reach an agreement with Max, then each of you does your part of it. Once that's happened, that's the end of the matter.'
3. 'If you and Max want to, you can build something into the agreement along the lines of "When all the terms are fulfilled, the parties agree that this matter is at an end".'
4. 'If it doesn't settle, then we'll talk about the next stage and you can decide what you want to do from there.'

For your client

Making an apology (during the mediation)

1. 'I'm sorry that matters have come this far, but I'd like to see if we can sort things out today.'
2. 'I'm sorry that you felt the need to complain. I'd like to understand your concerns.'
3. 'It sounds as though this whole matter has been stressful for you. I'm sorry about that. Let's talk about it so I can try to relieve some of that stress.'
4. 'I'm sorry that we seem to have fallen short of our normal high standards of service. Let's talk about how we can redress that.'
5. 'I realise I've made a mistake. I apologise for that and I'd like to work out how I can fix matters in the best way.'

Note

1. Example based on the real-life situation of Quentin Tarantino and his neighbour.

Appendix 1

Online dispute resolution

In the first edition of this book I did not include a section about online dispute resolution (ODR). However, the use of ODR has grown over recent years, so in my view it is important that lawyers are aware of it and of the benefits it can bring to clients.

In an article in 2001, the president of the American Arbitration Association predicted that the increasing use of e-commerce would lead to a growth in the use of ODR. William K. Slate II discussed the results of a B2B e-commerce survey carried out with 100 large organisations. In a world where the Internet is core to marketing, buying and selling, billing and inventory control, Slate writes, B2B companies

> will want to resolve matters online, have their complaint filed online, their documents considered online, their hearing held online, their decision rendered online, and be serviced by institutional providers.[1]

In 2010, the baton was taken up by the American Arbitration Centre, which introduced a paperless ODR programme to resolve disputes. While this programme was designed primarily as an alternative to full-blown arbitration, it is easy to see how it would transfer to a similar mediation style of dispute resolution:

> Manufacturers and suppliers are repeatedly involved in conflicts with each other that turn on a few essential questions of fact, such as what was ordered and what was delivered. These claims tend to be too small to resolve efficiently and cost-effectively in court or in regular commercial arbitration proceedings. For this reason, the parties need a streamlined alternative way to rapidly conclude these disputes without jeopardizing their business relationship.[2]

In 2012, I mediated a simulated dispute set up as part of a pilot programme sponsored by the Association for Conflict Resolution Hawaii Chapter. The pilot was under the auspices of the Virtual Mediation Lab founded by Giuseppe Leone. For the simulation, Giuseppe controlled the IT side from Hawaii, the parties were in Brazil and Israel, and I was in Scotland as the mediator. It was a fascinating experience, and I was surprised how quickly the interactions made it feel as though everyone was in the same room. You can see the award-winning performances on <https://www.youtube.com/watch?v=-neknWYzd8o> (last accessed 14 May 2016).

Before that simulation, I had undertaken a number of telephone mediations where one party is with me in a room with a hands-free phone and the other person is in a different location. Because there was no opportunity for those involved to see each other and read the nuances of body signals, it was never ideal. However, it can and does work.

The use of Skype and other technology platforms overcomes this hurdle. They can prove useful tools if the disputing parties are in different geographical locations, saving both time and money. On the Virtual Lab website there is a short video[3] explaining online mediation. While aimed primarily at mediators, it provides an informative description of the process which lawyers too may find beneficial.

The use of ODR has been enshrined in the EU by Directive 2013/11/EU. The aim of the Directive is to provide consumers with access to ADR for resolving disputes with traders, whether the transaction occurred online or not. The transaction can be for either a product or a service and it is irrelevant whether the trader is in the same Member State as the consumer or not. The only services excluded from the Directive are health and higher education.

Under the associated Regulation,[4] the European Commission has created a platform[5] for use by consumers and traders. This user-friendly process provides a gateway to dispute resolution by national ADR bodies for online transactions across the EU. In appropriate circumstances, you may find it useful to point your consumer clients to this site as an option for them to consider.

Clients who are online traders do not have to use ADR, but they are required to provide information about the option on their websites (if they have one). They must provide a link to the ODR platform and show their email address. For traders, the online platform provides the opportunity to avoid expensive litigation and to maintain good relationships with customers.

My aim in this appendix has been to alert you to ODR. It is not appropriate for me to try to explain all the niceties of the Regulations, so I leave that to your expertise!

Notes

1. Slate, 'Online dispute resolution', 12.
2. Altenkirk, 'A fast online dispute resolution program'.
3. <http://www.virtualmediationlab.com/virtual-mediation-lab-usa-international/online-mediation-explained-in-9-minutes/> (last accessed 15 May 2016).
4. Regulation (EU) No. 524/2013.
5. <http://ec.europa.eu/consumers/odr/>

Appendix 2

Documentation

What the mediator provides in advance of the meeting to either your client and/or you:

1. Contract for Services
2. Terms and Conditions
3. Draft Agreement to Mediate

What the mediator provides at the mediation:

1. Final Agreement to Mediate – one for each party and one for self
2. If no lawyers are present, the mediator usually writes up the terms of the Settlement Agreement as dictated by the parties. She leaves each with a copy and may or may not retain one herself.

What the lawyer provides in advance of mediation:

1. Summary for the mediator (see Chapter 6 – Logistics and other points)
2. If appropriate and if they will aid preparation for a fruitful discussion at the mediation, copies of relevant documents for the mediator and/or other party.

What the lawyer provides at the mediation:

1. Copies of any documents which may help discussion at the meeting
2. The Settlement Agreement reflecting the wishes and intentions of the parties (see Chapter 6 – Resolution).

Appendix 3

Sample Contract for Services

Mediation Scotland

It's your solution

This contract is between
Mediation Scotland
and
(Party A/Party B)
It is agreed as follows:
1. The mediation is between (Party A) and (Party B)
2. The fee payable in advance to Mediation Scotland is £
3. Known expenses payable in advance to Mediation Scotland are £
4. This contract includes the attached Costs, Terms and Conditions
5. This contract is governed by the laws of Scotland.

(Party A) or (Party B) acknowledges receipt of a copy of the Costs, Terms and Conditions.

....

(Party A) or (Party B)   Date

....

For and on behalf of Mediation Scotland   Date

Appendix 4

Sample Costs, Terms and Conditions

Mediation Scotland

It's your solution

Mediation Fees

The value of the dispute is based on the amount claimed or counter claimed, whichever is higher. In cases where no claim value can be clearly identified, or for workplace mediations, an estimate will be agreed prior to any costs being incurred.

Value of dispute	Fee per party per day or part day (plus VAT)	Outlays per party
Less than £10,000	£x	*If required*, equal share of additional costs such as room hire and catering, travel, accommodation for mediator(s)
£10,000–£30,000	£x	
£30,000–£100,000	£x	
More than £100,000 or no monetary value	By negotiation	

The fee includes

- pre-mediation discussions as deemed necessary by Mediation Scotland
- the provision of 1 or 2 mediators (at the sole discretion of Mediation Scotland)
- organising the mediation, including the venue and any other requirements
- all mediator preparation
- up to one full day of mediation
- any post-mediation feedback that is required.

The fee does not include

- the costs of an independent venue for the mediation, including room hire, catering, photocopying, telephone calls and other charges imposed by the venue

- any agreed abnormal travel costs, overnight accommodation or subsistence costs for the mediators.

Payment

An invoice will be issued to each party for the mediation fee and any known additional costs. This is payable no later than 14 days in advance of the mediation. Cleared funds must be received before the mediation starts.

If, following the mediation, there is any additional fee or costs due then a second invoice will be issued which is payable no later than 14 days from the invoice date.

Cancellation

In the event of cancellation in writing by any party after the mediation date has been confirmed, Mediation Scotland will be entitled to recover the following:

- If cancelled at least 14 days or more before the mediation date, any non-recoverable expenses and a £50 + VAT per each party cancellation charge, payable by the party/parties who cancelled.

- Less than 14 days but more than 7 days before the mediation date, any non-recoverable expenses and a £200 + VAT per each party cancellation charge, payable by the party/parties who cancelled.

- Less than 7 days but more than 24 hours before the mediation date, any non-recoverable expenses and 50 per cent of the total mediation fee + VAT cancellation charge payable by the party/ parties who cancelled.

- Less than 24 hours before the mediation date, any non-recoverable expenses and 100 per cent of the total mediation fee + VAT cancellation charge payable by the party/parties who cancelled.

Re-scheduled Mediations

If a mediation is cancelled and subsequently takes place at a date within 30 days of the original mediation date then no cancellation provisions will apply, other than for the non-recoverable expenses.

Sample Agreement to Mediate

Mediation Scotland

It's your solution

THIS AGREEMENT is between

1.	(Party A)
2.	(Party B)
3.	(Adviser to Party A)
4.	(Adviser to Party B)
5.	(Mediator)
6.	(Mediator)

} jointly 'the Parties'

Representatives of the Parties

Where a Party is a body, the Representative of a Party is the person appointed by the Party to attend the mediation on its behalf.

1.   (Party A Representative)
2.   (Party B Representative)

Advisers to the Parties

The Adviser (if any) to a Party is the legal or other adviser who attends the mediation to assist the Party.

1.   (Party A Adviser)
2.   (Party B Adviser)

Mediators

'The Mediator' is the person or persons named above. The Mediator acts as an independent contractor and is not an agent or employee of Mediation Scotland.

Mediation Scotland

The role of Mediation Scotland is to administer the mediation.

The mediation will take place at:
>Location
>Day Date
>Time

The Parties and all signatories agree as follows:

1. Each Party will attempt in good faith to resolve the dispute using the mediation process and will attend the mediation *with full authority to settle the dispute.*
2. The Parties have appointed the Mediator to mediate between them. The Mediator shall act as an independent, impartial facilitator and will not adjudicate, arbitrate, furnish legal or other advice, or impose a decision or solution in respect of any of the issues.
3. If, at the end of the meeting, the dispute remains unresolved the mediation session can be continued later if that is the wish of all the Parties, including the Mediator.

Procedure at the mediation

4. The Mediator will be responsible for conducting the mediation meeting in accordance with this Agreement and the Guidelines for Mediators, in consultation with the Parties.
5. No formal transcript or recording of the mediation will be made.
6. Any Party, Representative, Adviser or Mediator may withdraw from the mediation at any time.

Settlement

7. When/if the Parties agree to resolve the dispute, a Settlement Agreement will, if appropriate and required by the Parties, be prepared and signed by them or their Representatives.
8. In the event that a Party does not fulfil the terms of the Settlement Agreement, the other Party may be released from the settlement terms if they so wish, by giving written notice to that effect to the other Party;
9. All Parties to the dispute reserve their respective legal rights should a Settlement Agreement not be reached through mediation.

Confidentiality

10. The entire process of the mediation, including all communications prior to the mediation and all related documents, is and will be kept private and confidential.
11. The Mediator will not disclose to any Party or Adviser any information provided by another Party or Adviser in confidence without the express consent of the Party or unless required by law or public policy.
12. The mediation shall be treated as privileged and will be conducted without prejudice to any action in the courts. This paragraph shall not apply where:
    i. The Parties agree to specific disclosure;
    ii. Disclosure is necessary to implement and enforce the Settlement Agreement;
    iii. The Parties are, or any other person is, required by law to make disclosure;
    iv. A Party discloses anything that is unlawful.
13. The Mediator may not act for either Party individually in any capacity with regard to the subject matter of the mediation.

14. No Party, Representative or Adviser may have access to the Mediator's notes or call the Mediator as witness in any proceedings related to any of the issues between them. Unless directed by the Court, the Mediator's opinion will be inadmissible in any subsequent proceedings, which may take place between the Parties, Representatives or Advisers concerning the subject matter of the mediation.

Costs

15. The Parties agree to proceed on the basis of the standard terms and conditions of Mediation Scotland, including the mediation fee as previously agreed by the Parties and Mediation Scotland.
16. Each Party will be responsible for their own costs of representation.
17. Costs relating to court action may or may not be part of any Agreement, according to the wishes of the Parties.

Exclusion of liability

18. Neither the Mediator nor Mediation Scotland shall be liable to the Parties, Representatives or Advisers for any act or omission in connection with the services provided by them. However the Parties will have access to the Complaints Procedure of Mediation Scotland.

Applicable law

19. This Agreement to Mediate shall be governed by the laws of Scotland whose courts shall have exclusive jurisdiction.

The terms of this Agreement to Mediate, as set out above, are agreed and signed

--Date----------------------
For and on behalf of Party A
--Date----------------------
For and on behalf of Party B
--Date----------------------
Adviser to Party A
--Date----------------------
Adviser to Party B
--Date----------------------
Mediator
--Date----------------------
Mediator

Appendix 6

Sample Settlement Agreement and Joint Minute

(Example of an agreement made between the parties without legal advisers present at mediation.)

This agreement is between Mr Jimmy Bond trading as Expert Window Installers and Mr Maxwell Smart.

The parties agree that:

1. Jimmy will replace the three windows on the first floor of Max's house with ones shown in the attached brochure (item number 1245) by 31 March 2017.
2. Jimmy will clear all mess created by this replacement and will take all rubbish away with him.
3. On completion of the work, Max will pay Jimmy £530 in cash.
4. Jimmy will hand Max a receipt showing that this payment is in full and final settlement of invoice number 743.
5. Max will submit a Joint Minute (as attached) advising the court that Jimmy's claim against Max for £950 is to be withdrawn because they have settled the dispute through mediation.
6. Jimmy apologises for the stress and inconvenience he has caused Max.
7. Max will not write his intended letter to the local paper complaining about Jimmy's workmanship.
8. This agreement is in full and final settlement of the dispute between them.

....

Mr Jimmy Bond   Date
Trading as Expert Window Installers

....

Mr Maxwell Smart   Date

JOINT MINUTE

Case number SC 2589
Mr Jimmy Bond (trading as Expert Window Installers)
v
Mr Maxwell Smart

This case was set down for a further hearing on Monday 4 April 2017. The parties have reached resolution through mediation and now ask the court to discharge the action and grant Decree of Absolvitor with no expenses due to or by either Party.

Signed ....
Mr Jimmy Bond (trading as Expert Window Installers)

Signed ....
Mr Maxwell Smart

[*Note*. When I was managing the Edinburgh Sheriff Court Mediation Service, I would use a Joint Minute such as this to remove the case from the court list. The parties did not need to appear. I simply handed the signed Minute to the Sheriff Clerk once I knew that the terms of the Settlement Agreement had been fulfilled. A similar process may or may not be allowed in other jurisdictions.]

Checklist for choosing a mediator

Rapport building	
• Instils confidence in you	
• Feels trustworthy	
• Seems like the sort of person your client would respect	
Communication	
• Listens carefully	
• Doesn't interrupt you	
• Asks appropriate questions	
• Lets you do most of the talking	
• Explains process clearly	
• Discusses the pros and cons of mediation	
Recognises own limitations	
• Declines the work if not trained in that area	
• Acknowledges limits of own experience	
• If appropriate, discusses idea of another mediator	
Conflict of interest	
• Checks for any conflicts	
Organisational skills	
• Knows how to arrange logistics	
Additional support	
• Offers to send you further information	
• Offers to have a chat with your client/other solicitor	
Pricing	
• Provides you with a clear pricing structure	
Quality assurance	
• Initial training – at least 30 hours	
• Co-mediating with more experienced person – at least 6 hours	
• Which Code of Conduct followed	
• Complaints procedure in place	
• Level of professional indemnity insurance – at least £1 million	
Does this person feel 'right'?	
Notes	

Appendix 8
Checklist for preparation

BATNA/WATNA	Who	
• Ask 'If you aren't able to resolve this through mediation, what are the alternative options?'	Solicitor (S)	
• Think of some possible alternatives so that, if clients have difficulty getting off the mark, you can assist them	S	
• Write down all alternatives without initially assessing or criticising them	S	
• Provide legal advice as appropriate about the alternatives, once the list is complete	S	
• Start managing your clients' expectations	S	
• Think of alternatives to settlement	Client (C)	
• Decision about BATNA, either following or ignoring your advice	C	
• Discuss the alternatives	Both (B)	
Risk analysis		
• Prepare draft risk analysis sheet	S	
• Explain the purpose to your clients	S	
• Encourage them to include other people in the risk analysis preparation if appropriate	S	
• Provide advice about the likelihood of successfully proving relevant points in court	S	
• Advise amount of potential costs if the dispute is litigated	S	
• Help your clients differentiate between their stated positions and their real interests	S	
• Ask 'When this dispute is over, what do you want things to look like?'	S	

• Complete the risk analysis as much as possible, adding any other relevant considerations	C	
• Discuss and finalise the risk analysis	B	
• Discuss and use as part of strategy and tactics preparation	B	
Potential outcome analysis		
• Consider potential outcomes before discussing with your clients	S	
• Clarify in your own mind how you will explain financial calculations to them	S	
• Prepare a pro forma or memory-jogger to help you and your clients assess new options during private sessions at mediation (or for clients to use if you do not attend mediation with them)	S	
• Brainstorm potential outcomes, possibly using your initial thoughts as a starting point	B	
• Work through financials together so your clients understands their options	B	
• Use pro forma as suggested above	B	
Plasticine		
• Explain the idea to your clients	S	
• Demonstrate how to work it out	S	
• Provide information, for example cost of servicing, likelihood of a sale of their business at full price or reduced price	C	
• Work out what the BATNA represents and use it as part of strategic/tactical planning	B	
Decision analysis		
• Prepare flow chart of potential decision points before meeting with clients	S	
• Consider options which arose during the potential outcomes analysis	B	
• Discuss and adapt initial flow chart before the mediation	B	
• In private sessions during mediation, use flow chart as a working tool to aid consideration of options	B	

Logistics		
• Provide information for the mediator	S	
• Collate relevant documents and have copies ready	S	
• Ensure the 'right' people are at the table	S	
• Start managing your clients' expectations	S	
• Coach your clients as appropriate	S	
• Get a good night's sleep	B	
Opening statement		
• Tell your clients that the mediator will ask each party to make an opening statement	S	
• Guide your clients with the content	S	
• Advise your clients that it is their statements, so they should feel comfortable with what they are saying and how they are saying it	S	
• Clients should use their own words	C	
• They should ideally write them down or at least have bullet points to refer to	C	
• They should use non-inflammatory language	C	
• They should set the tone – conciliatory if possible	C	
• They should recognise different points of view	C	
• Decide who will make the opening statement (ideally the clients)	B	
• Consider tactics	B	

Assessing mediator performance

In Chapter 3, I described the flow of a mediation and warned that some of the points might sound pedantic. Below is the same description, but with added notes about *why* the words or actions are important. When you are assessing the mediator, you may wish to look out for these points as you build your opinion of her style and professionalism.

The parties or their lawyers have provided me with background information, so I've done my preparation. On the day there will be a minimum of two rooms available. *This is the normal situation. Sometimes the parties' budgets may be small, and so it may be necessary to use a second area such as a lounge area (in a hotel for instance). However, this is not ideal by any means as privacy may be compromised. The rooms should be sound-proof and roughly similar in size if possible. Many venues have adjacent meeting rooms. This in itself is not a problem, but I always check that conversations can't be overheard. If they can be, I would not use that room or, possibly, venue. If budgets and facilities allow, it is ideal to have three rooms. In this situation, each party has his own room and the third is used for joint meetings. Within the joint meeting room, I ensure that the table and chairs are arranged in the best possible way. By this I mean that I've either asked for a round table in advance or else I minimise the size of a rectangular arrangement as much as possible. I don't want to emphasise confrontation by having the parties physically miles apart. I move the chairs reasonably close to mine to create a collaborative atmosphere. I also point the parties' chairs towards mine rather than have them directly facing each other's.*

The parties usually arrive separately, so I greet them, offer refreshments and make small talk. *Most parties who attend mediation are doing so for the first time. No matter how worldly, professional or sophisticated they may be, most are anxious. I use this opportunity to set a tone of professionalism combined with informality to help them relax.*

Once the preliminaries are out of the way, I move the first party (let's call him Tim) into one of the rooms, point out where he should sit and leave him to it.

I direct Tim to a particular seat so that he does not choose a dominant place at the table. This is a subtle reinforcement that I as mediator control the process. I leave Tim at this point, so when Jack turns up he doesn't get the feeling that I might have been hearing Tim's side of the dispute first. The mediator must not only be impartial but be seen to be impartial at all times.

I wait outside the room for Jack (the other person) to turn up – greet, cuppa, weather discussion, and then invite him into the room where Tim is waiting. (While Jack's helping himself to coffee, I quickly pop in to tell Tim that Jack has arrived.)

I am demonstrating openness, keeping Tim informed and reinforcing my impartiality.

I guide Jack towards Tim.

I do this to encourage them to shake hands and to acknowledge each other as people, rather than as the source of their hassles.

I make the introductions.

Unbelievably, the parties sometimes have never met.

I then direct Jack to sit where I suggest.

As per my approach with Tim above.

Once everyone is settled, I thank them both for coming.

The purpose of this is to reassure them that they've made a good decision to come to mediation and to recognise that they have come voluntarily.

I cover any housekeeping.

This keeps them informed and demonstrates the importance of communication, subtly giving the message that we have to talk to each other rather than assume everyone knows the situation.

I then move quickly to the Agreement to Mediate. Both Tim and Jack will have received a draft copy of this from me in advance, with the invitation to contact me if they have any questions. For the meeting I have prepared final copies for us each to sign.

Signing at the same time and in the same place is an initial step towards doing things together. It is also a first point of agreement.

I check if either has any questions, and if not, I refer to the clause about confidentiality and remind them that this is key to the discussions at mediation. We sign three copies and retain one each.

I then explain my role in the process.

This is an opportunity to remind the parties that I am there to facilitate the discussion between them and manage the process. I give them a picture of possible success by referring to a written agreement at the end of the day. I provide an optimistic tone by mentioning the high 'success' rate of mediation.

I remind the parties that mediation is voluntary.

It is their meeting. I'll manage the process but they control the content.

I tell them we have two rooms available so if either wants a private discussion with me, we can use that.

Again, I demonstrate open communication and reinforce the point that my role is to help.

I will describe a possible flow for the day. For example: 'As I mentioned to each of you on the phone, I'd like to start by asking you to briefly tell the other how you see the situation between you, and most importantly how you would like to resolve your differences. While you're each having your say, I'd ask that the other person doesn't interrupt. So Tim, if Jack starts, I'd appreciate if you don't interrupt while he's speaking, and then vice versa for you, Jack, when it's Tim's turn. Do you both agree to that?

By asking this question, I am adding to the list of points about which they both agree.

Great, thanks for that. Once you've each had an opportunity to talk, then we can either stay together in this room or we can use both. We can play it by ear and see how things flow. Remember, do just say if you want a bit of breathing space or you want a private chat with me at any time. Does that sound all right?

Another point of agreement and nodding of heads.

Great, who'd like to start?

I may or may not ask this, depending on the individuals concerned. If I think that one party may perceive himself to be the stronger and that he may use this power to dominate proceedings, I may invite the 'weaker' party to speak first.

The time taken to get to this point is 5–10 minutes from when we're all seated.

Jack speaks, and I thank him but make no other comment. Tim speaks, ditto. I then thank them both for being so open and positive.

Here I am trying to create a positive tone. Even if the parties have been a bit negative or confrontational, I will focus on the positive.

I summarise what each has said.

Summarising is an important tool for mediators. I use it to let each party hear someone else's understanding of what he has said. It also allows Jack to hear Tim's version of events in someone else's words, and vice versa. Summarising also reassures both Tim and Jack that I've been listening to what each has said and that his point of view is valid in his own eyes.

The rest of the meeting depends on the individuals. Sometimes they will start discussing matters directly with each other. It could be that they are still unsure where to begin, so I might help them establish priorities. We could all stay together or move to separate rooms straightaway. If they do separate, the parties will often come back together at different stages. Sometimes they may stay apart for the rest of the mediation. Of course this is not ideal, but it may be the best in a particular situation. *This part of the meeting is enhanced by the experience of the mediator. There is no textbook answer as to when parties should separate or be together. A good mediator is alert to the ebb and flow of emotions and is aware when tension points are about to arise. An experienced mediator is able to sit back if the discussion between the parties is fruitful, and she does not intervene for the sake of it.*

If the parties reach an agreement, I help them develop a form of words and write them down. *If they do not have lawyers with them, I generally do the writing. The reason I do this is to reinforce my role as the neutral and to avert the possibility that one party may take control of the agreement. The fact that I am doing the actual writing relieves the parties of the responsibility of having to undertake a task they may never have done before.*

I continue to reinforce the point that this is their agreement and that I am simply the scribe. For example:

Me	Jack, you said that you are willing to re-paint Tim's front door. When would you be able to do that by?
Jack	I could do it within the next two weeks.
Me	Tim, is that OK with you?
Tim	Yes, that's fine.
Me	Great, let's put a date on that. So two weeks from today is the fourth of April, so shall I write 'Jack agrees to re-paint Tim's front door by the fourth of April'?
Jack and Tim	Yes.
Jack	Hang on. Tim, you need to get the paint in time for me to do that.

Me	Tim, how would you like to incorporate that into agreement?
Tim	How about we say that I'll have the paint available in two days' time and then Jack can do the painting any time within the next two weeks?
Me	Jack, is that OK with you?
Jack	Sounds good.
Me	So, shall I write 'Tim will get the paint by Thursday this week and Jack will re-paint the front door of Tim's house by the fourth of April'?
Jack and Tim	Yes, that'll do.

All the way through this I am reinforcing the point that the wording is theirs and this is a joint agreement which they own.

I will write this down and go through similar steps with the remaining terms. Once both Tim and Jack are satisfied, I read out the whole agreement to ensure both are still happy with what's written. Each signs this Settlement Agreement.

They demonstrate their commitment by signing in front of each other. (I generally have a laptop and printer with me at mediations. This allows me to give each party a signed copy to take with them.)

Once things are completed, I thank them again, remind them about confidentiality, discuss any follow-up steps and wave them off into the sunset.

If Tim and Jack were not able to reach agreement, I would bring the mediation to a close at an appropriate point. I thank them for trying, advise of next steps, reinforce confidentiality more strongly and then escort them to the exit individually. *Sometimes one will hang back or head out quickly, indicating that he doesn't want to have to walk out with the other party. I stay attuned to this so that neither is put in an awkward situation.*

This mediation will have lasted from as little as an hour to as long as ten hours, depending on the nature of the dispute.

Appendix 10

Checklist for assessing mediator performance

Logistics	
• Arranges suitable rooms	
• Provides suitable refreshments	
• Arranges table and chairs appropriately	
Rapport building	
• Sets appropriate atmosphere by meet and greet	
• Keeps parties informed	
Opening	
• Sets a positive tone	
• Encourages early agreement on small points	
• Demonstrates impartiality	
• Handles questions effectively	
• Advises on housekeeping and emergency procedures	
During	
• Listens effectively	
• Summarises appropriately	
• Talks as little as possible	
• Stays alert to emotions	
• Breaks when appropriate	
• Controls the process, not the content	
• Ensures each party has the opportunity to be heard and to listen	
• Stops inappropriate behaviour by a party	
• Instils confidence	
• Maintains impartiality	
• Does not offer opinions or advice	
• Treats parties equally and sensitively	
• Records Settlement Agreement appropriately	

Wrap	
• Reminds about confidentiality	
• Thanks parties for participating	
• Escorts each from the room	
Post-mediation	
• Follows through with any commitments promptly (e.g. sending copies of Settlement Agreement)	
• Writes to you to thank you for recommending her	
Would I use this mediator again?	
Notes	

Appendix 11

Assessing your own performance

Date of mediation	Client name
Length (hours)	Other party name
Brief description of dispute	
Stage of prior proceedings	
Outcome of mediation	
What I did well	
• In preparation	
• During the mediation	
• After the mediation	
What I want to remember for next time	
• In preparation	
• During the mediation	
• After the mediation	
Mediator name and contact details	
What did she or he do well?	
What could she or he have done better?	
Would I use this mediator again?	

Appendix 12
Client profiles and predicting the future

What is the age profile of your current client base? If a large percentage are in the latter stages of working life or already retired, how will you replace them over the coming years? Gone are the days where most people stayed with one employer all their lives. I would suggest that gone too are the days where clients are prepared to stay with one firm if it is not meeting their needs. Are you doing enough to retain this business? Are you doing enough to attract younger clients? What will your clients look like in the future?

In ten years' time, today's teenagers will be in their mid-twenties, hopefully in jobs, starting their own businesses, buying property and dealing with parents' estates. These future clients will probably suffer withdrawal if for five minutes they haven't sent a text, tweeted or emailed (or whatever new communication has evolved by then). They expect to receive responses quickly. If as adults they don't perceive similar outcomes from using your services, they may look elsewhere.

It may be tempting to think that there is plenty of time for you to adapt your practice to be able to offer the right services to these clients. However, remember back ten years. Has it passed quickly? How many different things have changed in your life for better or for worse? Did you plan these or did they just happen to you?

'Wise' people say you can't predict the future. I'm not sure I entirely agree with that. We *can* plan our futures and choose how we would like them to be. There is empirical evidence that planning, writing down and sharing our goals does help us achieve them. You may have read the oft-quoted studies of students from either Harvard or Yale Business School. (Supposedly, a study showed that students who wrote down their goals were more likely to have achieved them than those who simply verbalised them.) However, while this study did not actually happen, research *was* undertaken by Dr Gail Matthews, Psychology Professor at the Dominican University of California.[1] The 149 participants came from a variety of backgrounds, countries and age groups.

The study concludes:

1. The positive effect of accountability was supported: those who sent weekly progress reports to their friend accomplished significantly more than those who had unwritten goals, wrote their goals, formulated action commitments or sent those action commitments to a friend.
2. There was support for the role of public commitment: those who sent their commitments to a friend accomplished significantly more than those who wrote action commitments or did not write their goals.
3. The positive effect of written goals was supported: those who wrote their goals accomplished significantly more than those who did not write their goals.[2]

Perhaps now is the time to write down your goals for future client profiles, and to develop your plans and strategies to achieve these outcomes.

Notes

1. Matthews, *Goals Research Summary*.
2. Ibid., p. 3.

Appendix 13
Confidentiality and privilege

For most mediations, the points about confidentiality and privilege are straightforward – what is discussed at mediation stays at mediation. However, the purpose of this appendix is to alert you as a lawyer to some of the points which have arisen in subsequent litigation, and to some which still need clarification.

The second point first. Usually all those participating in a mediation sign the Agreement to Mediate at the start of the meeting. This Agreement includes clauses about confidentiality and this becomes a contractual obligation. See, for example, Appendix 5.

If I talk with parties before the mediation day, I always tell them that these discussions are confidential. However, at this stage nothing has been signed, so the discussions come under 'without prejudice' privilege. Depending on your particular client and the complexity of the dispute, you may find it appropriate to ensure that this confidentiality is agreed in writing and signed before the mediation day.

Similarly, you may wish to check that post-mediation-day exchanges are also covered by contractual obligations as we do at Mediation Scotland. Our Agreement to Mediate includes the words 'The entire process of mediation . . . is *and will be kept* private and confidential'[1] (emphasis added).

Now to some case law. In 2009, a mediator sought to set aside a witness summons requiring her to appear following a mediation between the parties. Mr Justice Ramsey in QBD Technology and Construction Court dismissed her application in this case because 'the interests of justice lie strongly in favour of evidence being given of what was said and done'.[2]

The background to this decision was that the parties ('FAL' and 'DEFRA') had participated in mediation in an effort to resolve a dispute following the foot and mouth outbreak in 2001. Subsequently, FAL (through its liquidator) brought proceedings seeking to set aside the Settlement Agreement reached at mediation, alleging that they entered into the agreement under economic duress. The parties waived their right to the confidentiality of mediation. The question arose as to whether they could call the mediator to give evidence. The court ruled that they were entitled to do so and DEFRA later served a summons on the mediator. She sought to have the witness summons set aside, relying on the confidentiality clause in the mediation agreement. (In this book, I refer to this as the Agreement to Mediate.)

After a lengthy consideration of precedent and academic writings, Ramsey J summarised his opinion in this area by saying:

> Therefore, in my judgment, the position as to confidentiality, privilege and the without prejudice principle in relation to mediation is generally as follows
>
> (1) Confidentiality: The proceedings are confidential both as between the parties and as between the parties and the mediator. As a result even if the parties agree that matters can be referred to outside the mediation, the mediator can enforce the confidentiality provision. The court will generally uphold that confidentiality but where it is necessary in the interests of justice for evidence to be given of confidential matters, the Courts will order or permit that evidence to be given or produced.
>
> (2) Without Prejudice Privilege: The proceedings are covered by without prejudice privilege. This is a privilege which exists as between the parties and is not a privilege of the mediator. The parties can waive that privilege.
>
> (3) Other Privileges: If another privilege attaches to documents which are produced by a party and shown to a mediator, that party retains that privilege and it is not waived by disclosure to the mediator or by waiver of the without prejudice privilege.[3.]

In his conclusion, however, he said that while the mediator could rely on the confidentiality part of the mediation agreement, this could be overridden if the interests of justice so demanded.

The case between FAL and DEFRA was discontinued before Ramsey J delivered his judgment. However, it has provoked debate subsequently as to whether there should be a 'mediation privilege'.

(Most of my colleagues and I always shred our notes after mediation. Given the number we undertake, I think it highly unlikely that we would be able to recall specific details of a particular mediation months or years after the event. Even if we were able to, my concern is that I would recall only the unusual points – for example, someone being aggressive towards another party – and not the general points of the discussion.)

Other courts have considered the effect of confidentiality and the 'without prejudice' rule in a number of cases. In 2006, the Technology and Construction Court had ordered experts to produce a joint report, which was referred to in a subsequent mediation. There was no Settlement Agreement at mediation, and later, the Court of Appeal was asked to rule whether or not the joint report was privileged. The Court concluded that simply because a document was introduced at mediation did not automatically mean it was privileged.[4]

In *Oceanbulk Shipping*, the issue before the Supreme Court was 'whether it is permissible to refer to anything written or said in the course of the without prejudice negotiations as an aid to the interpretation of the agreement'.[5] In concurring with the reasoning of Their Lordships, Lord Phillips stated:

> When construing a contract between two parties, evidence of facts within their common knowledge is admissible where those facts have a bearing on the meaning that should be given to the words of the contract. This is so even where the knowledge of those facts is conveyed by one party to the other in the course of negotiations that are conducted 'without prejudice'. This principle applies both in the case of a contract that results from the without prejudice negotiations and in the case of any other subsequent contract concluded between the same parties.[6]

In an interesting case in Canada,[7] the Supreme Court stated that a court

> must give effect to a confidentiality clause to which both parties have agreed, and that it is open to the parties to contract out of common law rules, including the exception to settlement privilege. Parties may desire that the protection of confidential information disclosed in the mediation process be broader than that afforded by the common law privilege, and disregarding this desire would undermine one of the main features that encourage parties to opt for this oft-used form of alternative dispute resolution.

In this particular case, however, the standard clause about confidentiality in the Agreement to Mediate did not afford the parties the right to exclude mediation documents from subsequent court proceedings.

These are just a few examples to alert you to the issues coming out of the confidentiality of mediation discussions and outcomes. It is likely that greater clarification will come from the courts over time.

Notes

1. Agreement to Mediate, clause 10, Appendix 5.
2. *Farm Assist* para. 53(5).
3. *Farm Assist* para. 44.
4. *Aird.*
5. *Oceanbulk* para. 6.
6. *Oceanbulk* para. 48.
7. *Union Carbide* para. 29.

Appendix 14

Dispute resolution clauses

Many large commercial contracts include an arbitration clause which briefly sets out how parties agree to handle future disputes. Ideally, a mediation clause should be included in contracts where arbitration is unlikely to be the appropriate dispute resolution option.

The clause need not be lengthy. It could be something like:

1. If a dispute arises about matters associated with this contract, the parties agree to try to resolve matters by using mediation.
2. The parties agree that unless the alleged breach of contract requires an urgent intervention, they will respond to the offer of mediation within 14 days.
3. The mediator will be selected jointly and will be chosen from a list of at least three people.
4. The parties agree that formal proceedings will not commence until mediation has been tried.

(It's so many years since I studied law that I won't pretend that the above wording is correct. I write it more as an example of the simplicity of a mediation clause.)

Appendix 15

Extra people at the meeting

For some types of mediation (such as court, workplace or complaints), a party may ask if he can bring a 'supporter' or colleague. For example, in workplace mediation, I am often asked if a union representative can attend. In such instances I make two points.

Firstly, mediation is the opportunity for those directly involved to discuss matters face to face. It allows one to tell the other how the dispute has affected him, and the other to listen. The idea of having a union official speaking on behalf of the member is not the point of mediation. However, it can be helpful for someone like a union rep or friend to hear what's discussed in joint session, so that he can lend support in private session.

Secondly, if the 'extra person' *is* prepared to attend as a supporter rather than as the 'voice', I always say I will check with the other party to see if he agrees to the person's presence. The reason for this is that mediation is voluntary. Parties are attending of their own free will and so should know in advance who is going to be at the meeting. If the request for an extra person is refused, then it is up to the first party to decide whether he still wants to proceed with mediation.

The mediator should explain to all exactly what role the extra person should play. At the start of the mediation, she should remind everyone of this:

> Ian, thank you for agreeing to David's colleague Jenny attending this meeting. Jenny, as I've already explained, the discussion today will be primarily between Ian and David and you've agreed that you will take a back seat. Is that still OK with everyone?

Or:

> Ian, thank you for agreeing to David's colleague Jenny attending this meeting. As we'd discussed, Jenny did the actual work on the programming so you agreed it might be useful if she contributed to the discussion as well. Is that still OK with everyone?

Mediations are held in private and the discussions are confidential. While this benefits the parties, it does make it more difficult for others to see mediation in practice. No matter how good a role-play is, it's not quite the same as seeing the ebb and flow of a real mediation, the emotions played out during the day or how the resolution is crafted. If you can ever take the opportunity to sit in on a mediation as an observer, I'd suggest that you grab it with both hands. The same applies to junior members of your staff. Increasingly, I receive requests for trainee solicitors to, for example, observe a mediation. The experience is usually invaluable for them, even though they spend the meeting sitting silently in a corner. (It benefits the trainees even more if you ask them to be particularly alert to certain points. For example, 'Please let me know how you think the opening statement was received.')

Appendix 16

Our multicultural society and mediation

As our immigrant population increases, so does the number of people for whom English is not their first language.

If this is the case for your client, mediation can prove beneficial if he would prefer not to struggle with the complexities and language of formal processes. Mediation allows a party to express his concerns, and for each to clarify understanding. The comparative informality can help your client relax without worrying whether he is breaching the protocol of a court or tribunal room.

If your client needs an interpreter for the mediation, you should advise the mediator, and either you or she must seek agreement to this from the other party. A professional interpreter must be quite clear about the role he is undertaking. He is not there to advise your client or make suggestions about the dispute. His presence is required only to translate the discussion. Either you or the mediator should ensure the interpreter understands this.

Sometimes the suggested interpreter may be a friend or relative. This adds another dimension. When I am talking to parties before mediation, I always double-check who will attend the meeting. As you are aware, mediation is voluntary. A party agrees to participate because he accepts the opportunity to discuss issues with the other. Each reserves the right to say who should be present. If the suggestion is that a relative attend as an interpreter and as a supporter, the other party should be entitled to have a friend or relative there as well if he wants to.

It's simply about everyone agreeing in advance who is attending and what role they will be playing.

There is another interesting aspect to mediations involving parties who come from different cultural backgrounds. There is sometimes a lack of understanding between them about the importance of matters such as saving face or the role of women. When you and your client are preparing for mediation, it is worth discussing any potential issues which may arise. (In a mediation between a young Korean couple and their former landlord, the husband refused to accept an offer of £400 because he wanted £401. It was important to him to be the one whose offer was accepted, rather than the other way round. The landlord was not prepared to budge, because his 'point of principle' was important to him.)

Styles of mediation

This book has focused solely on one particular type of mediation – facilitative. There are two other styles which are included here so you can see the differences – transformative and evaluative.

Facilitative

This is likely to be the style you encounter most frequently in your work as a lawyer. The reason is that a mediator using this approach works with the parties to help them have a fruitful discussion which ideally leads to some form of settlement agreement which ends the dispute.

As you have seen already, the mediator acts as an impartial third party, and while she is responsible for the flow of the meeting she does not give advice or make the decision about resolution. The mediator does not need to have expertise in the subject area of the dispute. She helps the parties remove the outer layers of the artichoke to get to the heart of the matter and their real interests. The focus is more on the way forward than on lengthy discussion of what's happened in the past.

Transformative

This style of mediation was developed by the delightfully-named Robert A. Baruch Bush and Joseph Folger in 1994.[1] In their view mediation can be used to transform people and their relationships. Rather than focusing on resolving the current problem, a transformative mediator helps the parties in two key ways – empowerment and recognition.

She plays a secondary role to the parties, seeking to empower them to understand their own goals and skills, which they can use to make their own decisions. The aim is to help both parties handle not only the current problem, but future ones as well.

The mediator encourages each party to recognise the other's point of view and to realise that it may be as valid as his own. Again, the idea is that from transformative mediation, the parties will continue to recognise that not everyone sees the world in the same way and the possibility of future conflicts will be reduced.

If out of these two tools – empowerment and recognition – a solution is found to the current problem, then well and good. However, for the mediator using a transformative style, the real goal is to help parties draw on their own skills and resources to change the way they deal with conflict. In many ways, the mediator here is more a counsellor or coach.

Evaluative

While it seems that this style is practised frequently in the USA, I am not aware of it being used much in the UK. In my view, the evaluative approach is not 'true' mediation.

In this style, the neutral person is asked to consider the legal points of the dispute, to point out the strengths and weaknesses of the arguments and to offer advice on how a judge or a jury may decide the outcome. By the very nature of it, the neutral person usually has knowledge of the relevant law and may be a lawyer or former judge. Rather than help the parties focus on their real interests, the goal is to assess the likely outcome of the arguments in court so that each can decide whether it would be more cost-effective to settle without litigation. While there may be a role for this assistance, I don't think it should be referred to as 'mediation'. However, others may disagree with me.

	Facilitative	Transformative	Evaluative
Goal	Solve the current problem	Empower the parties and encourage recognition of other's viewpoints so individuals are able to decide themselves how to solve the current problem and future ones	Point out the strengths and weaknesses of the legal arguments and assess what might come from litigation
Mediator	Impartial: directs the process; doesn't decide the outcome	Impartial: allows the parties to decide the issues and process; coach and counsellor	Tells the parties the strengths and weaknesses of the legal arguments they present
Focus	Underlying interests of parties and look to the future	Underlying interests of parties and analysis of the past	Is it more cost effective to settle or to litigate?

In my experience, many facilitative mediators use small parts of the transformative and evaluative styles as well. For example, in a workplace mediation, I might say something like: 'So Fred, from your point of view, when people are at work they should do their jobs and not spend a lot of time socialising. And Myrtle, for you it's important to get the job done but it's also good to chat to colleagues about other things. It sounds as though you have different views from each other's. Maybe it doesn't mean that one of you is right and one is wrong – maybe it just means you're different.'

In a court mediation, I might say: 'You say that the judge will believe you when you say you paid Tom in cash but you haven't got a receipt. Why do you think the judge will believe you and not Tom?'

The skill is to balance impartiality with helping parties to recognise the other's perspective, and to balance not giving advice with holding up a mirror.

Note

1. Baruch Bush and Folger, *The Promise of Mediation*.

Appendix 18
Historical background to mediation

Today's ADR practitioners help resolve conflict using skills developed from a wide spectrum of cultures, religions, political beliefs and social environments, possibly dating from as early as 1800 BC.

Traditionally, many societies resolved their disputes by involving everyone in the tribe. Each had the opportunity to talk and to state his point of view. In their book *A History of Alternative Dispute Resolution*[1] the authors touch briefly on its use by the Bushmen of the Kalahari and Hawaiian Islanders, among others. Still today a similar approach is used among communities of Australian aboriginals, who may also look to an experienced elder to act as adjudicator in disputes.

During the time of Confucius (551–479 BC) the philosophy was that harmony was all important. It was considered best to seek compromise to disputes. As James Wall notes, this continued through to the time of the Ming dynasty (1368–1644) and 'rulers actively encouraged village leaders and elders to solve petty disputes within and between families'.[2] This form of local resolution made sense, as it was often not feasible for parties to travel to a distant town where a more formal 'court' was available.

Religious leaders also encouraged the use of local resolution before resource to courts. The Bible warns: 'Come to terms quickly with your enemy before it is too late and he drags you into court.'[3] Not exactly the most conciliatory way of putting it, but as Matthew 5 verse 9 goes on to say, 'Blessed are the peacemakers: for they shall be called the children of God'.[4]

In the Jewish faith, there has long been an emphasis on informal resolution. Before using the judicial forum of the *Beth Din*, parties are encouraged to try informal resolution through mediation (*bitzua*) or arbitration (*p'sharah*). Even if the rabbis of the *Beth Din* are asked to intervene, the focus remains on reconciliation. As Rabbi Adam Berner points out, 'From a Jewish perspective, both in a halachic and a philosophic sense, mediation is an ideal process of conflict resolution'. He goes on to talk about the prime objective being dispute resolution and says, 'The Torah is more concerned with restoring social harmony than with arbitrating legal issues.'[5]

A similar belief exists for the Islamic faith. As Mohamed Keshavjee[6] said, the Holy Qur'ān incorporates the principle of trying to resolve disputes through forgiveness. Again there is a focus on peace and harmony and the use of discussion to sort out differences.

In England, following the Declaration of the Assize at Clarendon by Henry II in 1166, judges started to travel around the country to hear cases. This brought about the need for national laws to replace local customs and rules. The role of the local dispute resolution was reduced as visiting judges stamped their authority on the outcome. Formal resolution became the norm, but access to justice was often limited to those with the necessary resources. With the formality came an adversarial approach to dealing with disputes, so the outcome of legal action was usually a winner and a loser. Fine points of law eloquently expressed often led to judgments which some regarded as unfair.

The formal approach to justice persisted as the only option for centuries. Gradually, though, there was a recognition that this may not always be the best way to establish the facts and determine just solutions. As Professor of Law Carrie Menkel-Meadow writes in the opening line of an article:

> In this Essay I suggest the heretical notion that the adversary system may no longer be the best method for our legal system to deal with all of the matters that come within its purview.[7]

Her thoughts echo the sentiments of an earlier writer, Mauro Cappelletti, who looks at ADR within the context of access to justice. He discusses the philosophy that all should be 'entitled to representation and information', and says that this should be

> a philosophy which accepts alternative remedies and processes, in so far as such alternatives can help to make justice fair and more accessible.[8]

There has been a growing recognition around the world that there is a need for citizens to resolve issues in ways which do not necessarily involve expensive litigation affordable only by a few. A number of countries now have legislation devoted entirely to mediation, or incorporate it into other Acts, Regulations or procedures. Here are a few examples:

1. Australia
    a. Federal Court of Australia Act 1976
    b. Administrative Appeals Tribunal Act 1975
    c. Native Title Act 1993
    d. Corporations Act 2001
2. China – Peoples Mediation Act
3. USA – Uniform Mediation Act (last revised in 2003)
4. Bulgaria – Mediation Act 2004
5. Countries within the EU have, or are in the process of developing, regulations to comply with the EU Directive,[9] for example, the Cross-Border Mediation (Scotland) Regulations 2011

Notes

1. Barrett and Barrett, *A History of Alternative Dispute Resolution*.
2. Wall and Blum, 'Community mediation', 4.
3. Matthew 5 in *The Living Bible*.
4. King James version.
5. Berner, 'Divorce mediation'.
6. Keshavjee, *Alternative Dispute Resolution*.
7. Menkel-Meadow, 'The trouble with the adversary system', 5.
8. Cappelletti, 'Alternative dispute resolution processes', 295.
9. Directive 2008/52/EC.

European Code of Conduct for Mediators

This code of conduct sets out a number of principles to which individual mediators can voluntarily decide to commit, under their own responsibility. It is intended to be applicable to all kinds of mediation in civil and commercial matters.

Organisations providing mediation services can also make such a commitment, by asking mediators acting under the auspices of their organisation to respect the code. Organisations have the opportunity to make available information on the measures they are taking to support the respect of the code by individual mediators through, for example, training, evaluation and monitoring.

For the purposes of the code mediation is defined as any process where two or more parties agree to the appointment of a third party – hereinafter 'the mediator' – to help the parties to solve a dispute by reaching an agreement without adjudication and regardless of how that process may be called or commonly referred to in each Member State.

Adherence to the code is without prejudice to national legislation or rules regulating individual professions.

Organisations providing mediation services may wish to develop more detailed codes adapted to their specific context or the types of mediation services they offer, as well as with regard to specific areas such as family mediation or consumer mediation.

1 COMPETENCE AND APPOINTMENT OF MEDIATORS

1.1 Competence

Mediators shall be competent and knowledgeable in the process of mediation.

Relevant factors shall include proper training and continuous updating of their education and practice in mediation skills, having regard to any relevant standards or accreditation schemes.

1.2 Appointment

The mediator will confer with the parties regarding suitable dates on which the mediation may take place. The mediator shall satisfy him/herself as to his/her background and competence to conduct the mediation before accepting the appointment and, upon request, disclose information concerning his/her background and experience to the parties.

1.3 Advertising/promotion of the mediator's services

Mediators may promote their practice, in a professional, truthful and dignified way.

2 INDEPENDENCE AND IMPARTIALITY

2.1 Independence and neutrality

The mediator must not act, or, having started to do so, continue to act, before having disclosed any circumstances that may, or may be seen to, affect his or her independence or conflict of interests. The duty to disclose is a continuing obligation throughout the process.

Such circumstances shall include

- any personal or business relationship with one of the parties,
- any financial or other interest, direct or indirect, in the outcome of the mediation, or
- the mediator, or a member of his or her firm, having acted in any capacity other than mediator for one of the parties.

In such cases the mediator may only accept or continue the mediation provided that he/she is certain of being able to carry out the mediation with full independence and neutrality in order to guarantee full impartiality and that the parties explicitly consent.

2.2 Impartiality

The mediator shall at all times act, and endeavour to be seen to act, with impartiality towards the parties and be committed to serve all parties equally with respect to the process of mediation.

3 THE MEDIATION AGREEMENT, PROCESS, SETTLEMENT AND FEES

3.1 Procedure

The mediator shall satisfy himself/herself that the parties to the mediation understand the characteristics of the mediation process and the role of the mediator and the parties in it.

The mediator shall in particular ensure that prior to commence-
ment of the mediation the parties have understood and expressly
agreed the terms and conditions of the mediation agreement including in particular any applicable provisions relating to obligations of
confidentiality on the mediator and on the parties.

The mediation agreement shall, upon request of the parties, be
drawn up in writing.

The mediator shall conduct the proceedings in an appropriate
manner, taking into account the circumstances of the case, including
possible power imbalances and the rule of law, any wishes the parties
may express and the need for a prompt settlement of the dispute. The
parties shall be free to agree with the mediator, by reference to a set
of rules or otherwise, on the manner in which the mediation is to be
conducted.

The mediator, if he/she deems it useful, may hear the parties
separately.

3.2 Fairness of the process

The mediator shall ensure that all parties have adequate opportunities
to be involved in the process.

The mediator if appropriate shall inform the parties, and may
terminate the mediation, if:

- a settlement is being reached that for the mediator appears
  unenforceable or illegal, having regard to the circumstances of
  the case and the competence of the mediator for making such
  an assessment, or
- the mediator considers that continuing the mediation is unlikely
  to result in a settlement.

3.3 The end of the process

The mediator shall take all appropriate measures to ensure that any
understanding is reached by all parties through knowing and informed
consent, and that all parties understand the terms of the agreement.

The parties may withdraw from the mediation at any time without
giving any justification.

The mediator may, upon request of the parties and within the lim-
its of his or her competence, inform the parties as to how they may
formalise the agreement and as to the possibilities for making the
agreement enforceable.

3.4 Fees

Where not already provided, the mediator must always supply the parties with complete information on the mode of remuneration which he intends to apply. He/she shall not accept a mediation before the principles of his/her remuneration have been accepted by all parties concerned.

4 CONFIDENTIALITY

The mediator shall keep confidential all information, arising out of or in connection with the mediation, including the fact that the mediation is to take place or has taken place, unless compelled by law or public policy grounds. Any information disclosed in confidence to mediators by one of the parties shall not be disclosed to the other parties without permission or unless compelled by law.

The approval of this code of conduct in 2004 led to the European Parliament and Council adopting Directive 2008/52/EC of 21 May 2009 on certain aspects of mediation in civil and commercial matters.

Case Studies

These are based on real mediations. To preserve confidentiality, I have changed the names (obviously) and have taken lots of liberties with the facts. The aim of these case studies is to give you an idea of the types of disputes and conflicts which have been mediated.

Claim by tenant for the deposit held by the landlord

Angus was a student who rented a flat from Rosa. At the end of the tenancy, Angus asked for his deposit of £500 to be returned to him. Rosa sent him a cheque for £100 with a letter saying that she was retaining the balance because Angus had left the flat in a mess and that there was a coffee-cup stain which couldn't be removed from the kitchen table.

Angus said that he had cleaned the flat before he left and that the stain was just part of general wear and tear. When Rosa refused to refund the balance of £400, Angus raised a Small Claims action in the Sheriff Court. When both parties appeared in court for the first hearing, the Sheriff referred the case to mediation. During the joint meeting, Rosa was able to show Angus photos of the flat after he had left it and a detailed invoice from a cleaning firm. At that stage the parties moved into separate rooms and the mediator met first with Angus.

In the private session, Angus said that perhaps his cleaning skills may not have been good enough to allow a new tenant to move in immediately. However, in his opinion the carpet did not need steam-cleaning and that just a good vacuuming would have been enough. He also pointed out that it was unfair to charge him for replacing four tiles in the bathroom, because they'd been broken when he moved in.

The mediator then spoke privately with Rosa, who realised that a Sheriff might consider the coffee-cup stain to be wear and tear and just one of the things that can happen when someone has been living in a flat for a year. She also realised that it could be difficult to prove that the tiles were broken by Angus. After further discussion, both Angus and Rosa decided that it could be stressful and time-consuming to go back to court. Between them they decided that Angus would be responsible for the cost of the work by the cleaning firm, and Rosa would bear the cost of the tiles and the coffee stain. Rosa agreed to refund Angus a further £75 of his deposit.

Dispute following the sale of a family business

Four siblings had started and built up a successful business, which they sold after five years. The contract for sale provided for an immediate lump sum payment, followed by annual payments for two years, based on the turnover of the business. One sibling, John, remained working with the new owners and was responsible for distributing the payments to his brothers and sisters.

John made an initial distribution shortly after the sale, but for unexplained reasons retained part of the funds. Over the next three years, the other siblings made repeated requests for further payments and an accounting of all figures. John released some funds, but said he was unable to provide accounting because of pressure of work and difficulties at home.

Before mediation, the other siblings had not spoken to John for four years. Gatherings at the family home were chilly and uncomfortable, and the elderly parents were increasingly upset at the discord among their children.

In the lead-up to the meeting, the mediator acted as an intermediary to pass financial information, questions and answers among the parties. This enabled everyone to have a better understanding of some of the figures before they met together. It also ensured that no one was caught out by an unexpected request for particular figures during the mediation.

The day started rather stiffly with one party deciding not to make an opening statement. Each sibling had different ideas about what he or she wanted to reveal, and this proved frustrating for the others at times. There were some angry scenes and lots of emotion, but overall recognition that this was probably their last chance to try to sort things out.

The flow of the mediation moved between joint meetings with all involved, separate discussions between two or three siblings, and individual sessions with the mediator. It was a long, intense day, which did not end in a final Settlement Agreement. The reason for this was that outstanding information was needed before final distributions could be calculated. However, the parties left with a comprehensive

Memorandum of Understanding which specified who was to do what and by when. They also agreed to contact the mediator again if they felt another meeting was needed to reach a formal agreement.

Was this mediation successful? In my view it was. More importantly, in the parties' views it was too. The siblings spent the whole day together and talked with each other for the first time in many years. Issues were put on the table, some venom spat and apologies made. Each began to recognise that there were different understandings of the same situation or conversation. Dogmatic views of the rights and wrongs were relaxed as the day progressed.

What worked well? The preparation by all concerned was critical to the progress made on the day. In addition, the siblings participated voluntarily, and each wanted to sort things out for peace of mind, and especially for the sake of their parents. The fact that as mediator I did not push for a final agreement on the day was important. Everyone was tired after eight hours, so I suggested they have the Memorandum of Understanding at that stage. The parties recognised that final resolution that day was not practical, so over the next two hours they developed the Memorandum to capture the points agreed and the next steps to be taken.

Will they finally resolve all the issues among them? I may never know. But what I do know is that the foundations for agreement have been laid. Each has a better awareness of what the others have been through over the past years, and they know that what their relationship will be like in the future is their choice.

Dispute over failure to maximise profits

Hamish was the brother of Tom, who died a year ago without leaving a will. Sally had been the partner of Tom for more than twenty years. Tom had owned a successful bicycle shop while Sally worked at the local bank.

After Tom's death, Sally tried to keep the shop running while still doing her own job. Although she and Tom had discussed business issues, she had never been involved in the day-to-day work. After a key manager resigned, Sally struggled to keep the business going, but she was able to make a small profit.

In the meantime Sally searched for Tom's will (she had seen a photocopy many years earlier which showed that his estate was left to her). When she was unable to find one, Hamish made a successful application to the court, which resulted in him inheriting Tom's estate, leaving Sally with nothing. The very next day, Hamish went to the bicycle shop and announced he was taking it over.

Hamish then brought an action against Sally, claiming that she had failed to keep the business running properly, causing a substantial drop in profits, and that she had taken stock which was not rightfully hers.

Both parties' lawyers attended mediation with their clients. Sally also had her accountant available in another room so he could answer questions relating to the financials.

This was an interesting mediation as it involved large sums of money, but the latent emotions played a more significant role. It became apparent that Hamish and his parents had always loathed Sally and felt that she had taken Tom away from them. Tom was considered the golden boy of the family, and they thought that Sally 'wasn't good enough for him'. Sally had not really had the opportunity to grieve for her partner because she had been flung into the business and the various legal actions straight after his death. In addition she was in a weaker financial position than Hamish, so could ill afford to lose in court.

The parties were able to resolve matters after two days. Hamish withdrew his allegations that Sally had stolen goods from the shop and a settlement figure was negotiated over the loss of profits; each realised that the other had loved Tom, and wanted to draw a line under this dispute because of him.

Complaint about poor service provided by a solicitor to a client

The complainer, Ms Unusualname, made a formal complaint against a firm of solicitors who had dealt with her father's estate. Part of the complaint was about unnecessary delays, and another was about the way she had been treated by members of staff of the firm. The parties agreed to mediate to try to resolve the complaint, rather than progress to a formal investigation.

When Ms Unusualname made her opening statement, she told the Client Relations Partner (CRP) of the firm how upsetting she had found the whole process. While she touched on the delays, her main concern was about the way a particular member of staff had been abrupt with her. She also revealed that her father's death meant she was the only person left with the unusual surname. This was an emotional point for her.

In response, the first thing the CRP did was to apologise for the upset that she felt. He then went on to tell Ms Unusualname that he had already spoken to staff in all the offices of the firm. He'd reminded them that, although they might deal with deceased estates on a daily basis, it is often the first time a client is facing the experience, which is made worse by sadness and grief at the death.

This apology, and demonstration that action had already been taken to reduce the possibility of recurrence, set a positive tone for the mediation. The parties discussed the firm's expectations of its staff, the client's perception of correspondence and phone calls, and, finally, the cause of the delays. In addition, the CRP acknowledged how the complainer felt about being the last in the family line. She was visibly relieved to realise that he seemed to understand how important this was to her.

The Settlement Agreement recorded the apology, the firm made a small financial payment to Ms Unusualname, and she withdrew her complaint. Mediation provided the opportunity for the complainer to talk face to face with someone who was prepared to listen. The CRP gained a better insight into how the firm can provide good service which helps retain clients. This mediation lasted for one hour.

Workplace mediation to smooth the way for return to work

Julie had been off work for six months on stress-related leave following ongoing difficulties with her manager, Gary. The company's HR manager had been in touch with Julie during her absence and together they had agreed a date for her to return to work. Mediation was arranged so Julie and Gary could discuss how they wanted their working relationship to look in the future.

Gary was extremely anxious as the beginning of the mediation. I had already spoken to both parties on the phone and talked with them about the confidentiality of the process. On the day I reminded them both again about this and reassured Gary that I wasn't going to be reporting anything back to his boss. Once he realised the truth of that, he became more relaxed and open to listening to points made by Julie. Some of these included past actions by Gary which Julie had interpreted as 'picking on her'.

As with so many disputes, the strained relationship had come about because of poor communication. Words had been interpreted differently from their intended meaning; other employees had passed on inaccurate gossip which had been taken as truth; assumptions had been made; actions had been misunderstood.

With the positive atmosphere of mediation, Julie and Gary began to acknowledge their differences and plan ways in which they could work effectively together. They reached an agreement which both felt laid a strong foundation for the future. Knowing that all good plans can go awry, I encouraged them to build in ways to deal with future issues before they grew. Thus Julie and Gary left the meeting with a better understanding of each other, a willingness to work together and a mechanism to help them deal with future niggles.

Postscript. It wasn't until I was reviewing my own performance as mediator that I realised that it was highly likely Julie couldn't read. If that were true, she had managed to cope with the reading part of her work without revealing the situation. This may have contributed to some of the difficulties she had with Gary. If I had twigged this during the mediation, I might have (sensitively) broached it in private session. We might then have discussed how she wanted to deal with this. Perhaps I could have helped her more. Hindsight's a wonderful thing, isn't it?

Action seeking compensation for reduced sale price of commercial premises

Green Limited had brought an action in the Court of Session against Save our Yellow Canaries charity ('Canaries'). Canaries had rented office premises from Green for a number of years. The lease agreement contained dilapidations provisions which required Canaries to ensure that the premises were restored to the original state at the end of the term. Canaries had failed to undertake the necessary work. Green alleged that this adversely affected the sale price which it eventually obtained.

Lawyers were with their clients throughout the mediation, but most of the discussion was between the representatives of Green and Canaries. It seemed that Green was on fairly strong ground legally, but the CEO had recognised that even if they were successful in court the chances of recouping the full amount of the claim from a charity were low.

So was this just a negotiation, or was it a mediation? I regard it as mediation (of course I would, I hear you say.). 'Normal' negotiations had been tried already and hadn't worked. Canaries had basically said it didn't have the money to pay, so Green could go jump. By choosing the option of mediation, both parties were able to sit down together and work out a solution to a problem that was not going to go away.

The Settlement Agreement was drawn up by the two lawyers after their clients had advised them of the terms they wanted to include. The result? Green recouped some of the money it was seeking. Canaries was able to pay by affordable instalments. Could Green have gone to court and won? Possibly yes, but the CEO realised it may have been a hollow victory. Better to make a smart commercial decision and accept a known amount. For Canaries, the outcome relieved concerns about court costs which it couldn't afford and the inevitable dissolution of the charity which would have resulted. This mediation lasted ten hours, with the last two being taken by the lawyers drafting the Settlement Agreement.

Dispute between business partners where working relationship had broken down

This was an interesting situation in which two colleagues had set up a very successful business some years previously. However, the relationship had soured and the colleagues knew that they had to part ways. The difficulty was that each wanted to be the one who retained the business. The mediation started as 'How do we sort out the split?' but moved to one of 'How are we going to be civil to each other, keep the business running and later work out the legalities of the split with our lawyers?'.

Emotions ran high during the day, with each refusing to consider the other's point of view for most of the time. Eventually, positive though wary dialogue started. The parties reached a Settlement Agreement which covered the behaviours of each in the lead-up to the legalities. The actual split of the business was not considered further at mediation.

This day was indicative of the flexibility of mediation. With my support, the parties were able to get to the heart of the issues between them. They were not locked in to having to deal with the business itself at that time, but were free to start breaking down the barriers between them so they could have effective further discussions about the future of the company.

Appendix 21
Useful references

Subject area

(All online material last accessed in May 2016)

Apology

Lazare, A. (2005) *On Apology* (Oxford: Oxford University Press).

Scott, V. (2010) '*I'm Sorry You're Such a Crybaby' Isn't Really an Apology*, <http://www.mediate.com/articles/scottV2.cfm>

Vines, P. (2008) 'Apologies and civil liability in England, Wales and Scotland: the view from elsewhere', *Edinburgh Law Review*, vol. 12, May, pp. 200–30.

BATNA/WATNA

Fisher, R. and W. Ury (1991) *Getting to Yes* (New York: Penguin), 2nd edn.

Notini, J. (2005) *Effective Alternatives Analysis in Mediation: 'BATNA/WATNA' Analysis Demystified*, <http://www.courts.ca.gov/partners/documents/batna_watna.pdf>

Confidentiality and privilege

Goodman, A. (2008) 'Privilege in the contents of mediation and round table meetings: paper walls?', *1 Chancery Lane*, vol. 2, issue 3, September, <http://1chancerylane.com/download/MTU2>

Kallipetis, M., 'Mediators awake'. [Originally published in *The Mediator Magazine*. Worth trying to find through a search engine, as it may resurface in the future.]

Wood, W., 'Farm Assist: mediators get another case of disclosure?'. [Originally published in *The Mediator Magazine*. Worth trying to find through a search engine, as it may resurface in the future.]

Wood, W., 'When girls go wild'. [Originally published in *The Mediator Magazine*. Worth trying to find through a search engine, as it may resurface in the future.]

Construction

Agapiou, A. and B. Clark (2010) *An Investigation of Construction Lawyer Attitudes to the Use of Mediation in Scotland*, COBRA conference, Paris, <https://www.irbnet.de/daten/iconda/CIB20090.pdf>

Agapiou, A. and B. Clark (2011) 'Scottish construction lawyers and mediation: an investigation into attitudes and experiences', *International Journal of Law in the Built Environment*, 3(2) IJLBE 159.

Gould, N., C. King, A. Hudson-Tyreman, J. C. Betancourt, P. Ceron, C. Lugar, J. Luton, A. K. Moecksch and Yanqiu Li (2009) *The Use of Mediation in Construction Disputes*, Her Majesty's Court Service and Kings College London, <http://www.fenwickelliott.com>

Gould, N., C. King and P. Britton (2010) *Mediating Construction Disputes: An Evaluation of Existing Practice*, Kings College, London, Centre of Construction Law and Dispute Resolution, <http://www.fenwickelliott.com>

Richbell, D. (2008) *Mediation of Construction Disputes* (Oxford: Blackwell).

Dispute resolution options and timing

Carper, D. L. (2008) 'What parties might be giving up and gaining when deciding not to litigate: a comparison of litigation, arbitration and mediation', *Dispute Resolution Journal*, vol. 63, issue 2, May–July, pp. 48–60.

International Institute for Conflict Prevention & Resolution (2005) *CPR European Mediation and ADR Guide*, <http://www.cpradr.org/Portals/0/20151116CPREABMediationGuide.pdf> [Useful overview of ADR processes with some practical advice about mediation and arbitration.]

Peters, R. J. and D. B. Mastin (2007) 'To mediate or not to mediate: that is the question', *Dispute Resolution Journal*, vol. 62, issue 2, May–July, pp. 14–21.

Sander, F. and S. B. Goldberg (2007) 'Fitting the forum to the fuss: a user-friendly guide to selecting an ADR procedure', in S. B. Goldberg and others, *Dispute Resolution: Negotiation, Mediation, and Other Processes* (Austin: Wolters Kluwer), 5th edn, pp. 337–50. [A useful essay on impediments to settlement and ways to overcome them.]

Guides

Chartered Trading Standards Institute, *Alternative Dispute Resolution* [guide for traders], <https://www.businesscompanion.info/en/quick-guides/consumer-contracts/alternative-dispute-resolution>

NHS Litigation Authority, *The Clinical Disputes Forum's Guide to Mediating Clinical Negligence Claims V1.07ii. July 2001*, <http://www.nhsla.com/Claims/Documents/Clinical Disputes Forum Guide.doc>

NHS Litigation Authority, *The Clinical Dispute Forum's Users' Guide to Mediation V1.02 July 2001*, <http://www.nhsla.com/Claims/Documents/Clinical%20Disputes%20Forum%20Guide.doc>

NHS Litigation Authority, *Mediation Leaflet*, <http://www.nhsla.com/CurrentActivity/Documents/Mediation%20Leaflet.pdf>

The Scottish Government (2009) *A Guide to the Use of Mediation in the Planning System in Scotland*, <http://www.gov.scot/Resource/Doc/263432/0078790.pdf>

History

Barrett, J. T. and J. P. Barrett (2004) *A History of Alternative Dispute Resolution* (San Francisco: Jossey-Bass).

Cole, S. D. (1902) 'English Borough Courts', *18 Law Quarterly Review 376*, pp. 380–2.

Mediation styles

Baruch Bush, R. and J. Folger (1994) *The Promise of Mediation: Responding to Conflict through Empowerment and Recognition* (San Francisco: Jossey-Bass).

Spangler, B., *Transformative Mediation*, <http://www.beyondintractability.org/essay/transformative-mediation> [While this article is informative, in my view the comparison of transformative and problem-solving mediation should be read as the 'idealized descriptions', as the author notes himself.]

Mediators

Goldberg, S. B. (2005) 'The secrets of successful mediators', *Negotiation Journal*, vol. 21, issue 3, July, pp. 365–76.

Goldberg, S. B. and M. L. Shaw (2007) 'The secrets of successful (and unsuccessful) mediators continued: Studies Two and Three', *Negotiation Journal*, vol. 23, issue 4, October, pp. 393–418.

Salomon, C. T. (2006) 'Selecting a mediator in international disputes: dare we speak of mediation as "winnable"?', *Dispute Resolution Journal*, vol. 61, issue 2, May–July, pp. 68–73.

Negotiation

Fisher, R. and W. Ury (1991) *Getting to Yes* (New York: Penguin), 2nd edn.

Thompson, L. T. (2005) *The Mind and Heart of the Negotiator* (Harlow: Pearson Education), 3rd edn.

Online Dispute Resolution

Altenkirk, M. (2012) 'A fast online dispute resolution program to resolve small manufacturer–supplier disputes', *Dispute Resolution Journal*, vol. 67, issue 3, August–October, pp. 48–53.

European Commission, *Settling Consumer Disputes Online*, <http://ec.europa.eu/consumers/solving_consumer_disputes/docs/adr-odr.factsheet_web.pdf> [Simple fact sheet.]

Fernandez, A. J. and M. E. Masson (2014) 'Online mediation: advantages and pitfalls of new and evolving technologies and why we should embrace them', *Defense Counsel Journal*, October, pp. 395–403.

Goldberg, J. (2014) 'Online Alternative Dispute Resolution and why law schools should prepare future lawyers for the online forum', *Pepperdine Dispute Resolution Law Journal*, vol. 14, pp. 1–25.

Slate, William K. II (2002) 'Online dispute resolution: click here to settle your dispute', *Dispute Resolution Journal*, vol. 56, issue 4, November 2001/January 2002, pp. 8–14.

Other

Acland, A. F. (1990) *A Sudden Outbreak of Commonsense* (London: Hutchinson Business Books).

Apple, R. (2013) 'Mediation offers less costly way to resolve disputes', *Physician Executive Journal*, November–December, pp. 60–3. [Article in relation to healthcare.]

Attree, R. (ed.) (2016) *Alternative Dispute Resolution: A Brief International Guide* (Libralex E.E.I.G.), <http://www.libralex.com/publications/alternative-dispute-resolution-brief> [Useful snapshot of the use of ADR in a number of European countries.]

Belyaeva, A. (2015) 'Prospects of the development of the mediation institute in the Russian Federation', *Dispute Resolution Journal*, vol. 70, no. 3, pp. 131–9. [An interesting look at the challenges facing mediation.]

Berner, Rabbi A. (1997) 'Divorce mediation: gentle alternative to a bitter process', *Jewish Law*, <http://www.jlaw.com/Articles/berner.html>

Brown, H. and A. Marriott (2011) *ADR Principles and Practice* (London: Sweet & Maxwell), 3rd edn.

Cappelletti, M. (1993) 'Alternative dispute resolution processes within the framework of the world-wide access-to-justice movement', *56 Modern Law Review* 282.

Court of Session (2009) *Report of the Scottish Civil Courts Review*, Vol. 1, <http://www.scotcourts.gov.uk/docs/default-source/civil-courts-reform/report-of-the-scottish-civil-courts-review-vol-1-chapt-1---9.pdf?sfvrsn=4>

Duncan, C. (2013) 'Mediation in the oil and gas industry: taking the best for the future', *Dispute Resolution Journal*, vol. 68, issue 4, pp. 7–85.

Federation of Law Societies of Canada, *Model Code of Professional Conduct*, www.flsc.ca

Federation of the Swiss Watch Industry FH, <http://www.fhs.ch/eng/watchindustrytoday.html>

Fleming, Neil D. and C. Mills (1992) *Not Another Inventory, Rather a Catalyst for Reflection*, To Improve the Academy, Paper 246, University of Nebraska–Lincoln, <http://digitalcommons.unl.edu/podimproveacad/246>

Gathier, E. (2010) *The Situation Regarding Mediation in The Netherlands*, presentation to Congreso Internacional de Mediación, Santiago de Chile.

Goldberg, S., F. Sander, N. Rogers and S. Rudolph Cole (2007) *Dispute Resolution: Negotiation, Mediation, and Other Processes* (Austin: Wolters Kluwer). [A comprehensive reference, but the focus is on the USA.]

Hanger, I. (2000) 'Senior executive appraisal mediation', *ADR Bulletin*, vol. 3, no. 4. Art. 1, pp. 45–7. [Description of a mediation process useful for large organisations in dispute.]

Henderson, J. (2008) 'The Federal Court's judicial nudge: court-ordered mediation', *QLS Journal*, July, <www.qls.com.au/files/8eac9a4c-72ef-406d-b1e6.../2_-_joshhenderson.pdf>

Irvine, C. (2012) 'Mediation: business as usual', *The Journal of the Law Society of Scotland*, 16 April, <http://www.journalonline.co.uk/Magazine/57-4/1011021.aspx>

Keshavjee, M. M. (2002) *Alternative Dispute Resolution: Its Resonance in Muslim Thought and Future Directions*, speech given as part of the Ismaili Centre Lecture Series, <http://akdn2stg.prod.acquia-sites.com/sites/default/files/keshavjee_adr-144515351.pdf>

Law Business Research Ltd (2015) *Mediation 2015: Trends*, <http://whoswholegal.com/news/analysis/article/32479/mediation-2015-trends/>

Law Reform Commission of Ireland (2008) *Consultation Paper on Alternative Dispute Resolution*, <http://www.lawreform.ie/_fileupload/consultation%20papers/cpadr.pdf>

Law Society of New South Wales (2012) *Dispute Resolution Kit, December 2012*, <https://www.lawsociety.com.au/cs/groups/public/documents/internetcontent/675694.pdf> [An easy read, and practical.]

Law Society of Scotland, Guidance related to Rule B1.9, <www.lawscot.org.uk>

Legal Ombudsman Business Plan (2010), <http://www.legalombudsman.org.uk/downloads/documents/publications/Business-Plan-2010.pdf>.

Lewicki, R. J., D. I. McAllister and R. J. Bies (1998) 'Trust and distrust: new relationships and realities' *Academy of Management Review*, vol. 23, no. 3, pp. 438–58.

Lord Chancellor's Department (1996) *Access to Justice: Final Report*, <http://webarchive.nationalarchives.gov.uk/+/http://www.dca.gov.uk/civil/final/sec2a.htm>

Malcolm, E. and F. O'Donnell (eds) (2009) *A Guide to Mediating in Scotland* (Dundee: Dundee University Press).

Matthews, G. *Goals Research Summary*, <www.dominican.edu/academics/ahss/psych/faculty/fulltime/gailmatthews/researchsummary2.pdf>

McKnight, H. D., L. L. Cummings and N. L. Chervany (1998) 'Initial trust formation in new organizational relationships', *Academy of Management Review*, vol. 23, no. 3, pp. 473–90.

Menkel-Meadow, C. (1997) 'The trouble with the adversary system in a postmodern, multicultural world', *William and Mary Law Review*, 5, 1996–7, pp. 5–44.

Menon, S. (2016) *Shaping the Future of Dispute Resolution and Improving Access to Justice*, Global Pound Conference Series 2016 – Singapore, <http://singapore2016.globalpoundconference.org/post-conference/content-results#.VzdhzzArLaY>

Newman, D. C. (2013) 'A creative industry needs a creative solution', *Dispute Resolution Journal*, vol. 68, issue 3, pp. 71–80.

Nolan-Haley, J. (2008) 'Consent in mediation', *14 Dispute Resolution Magazine*, 2007–8, p. 4.

Phillips, G. F. and V. Ignacio (2000) 'Entertainment industry recognizing benefits of mediation', *17 Ent. & Sports Law 29*.

Roberts, S. and M. Palmer (2005) *Dispute Processes: ADR and the Primary Forms of Decision-Making* (Cambridge: Cambridge University Press), 2nd edn.

Rogers, N. and R. Salem (1993) *A Student's Guide to Mediation and the Law* (New York: Matthew Bender).

Ross, W. H. (2000) 'Hybrid forms of third-party dispute resolution: theoretical implications of combining mediation and arbitration', *Academy of Management Review*, vol. 25, no. 2, pp. 416–27.

Scottish Government (2016) *Civil Justice Statistics in Scotland 2014–2015* <http://www.gov.scot/Resource/0049/00497242.pdf>

Solicitors Regulation Authority, *Code of Conduct*, Chapter 1, Client Care: O (1.12), <www.sra.org.uk>

Wall, J. A. and M. Blum (1991) 'Community mediation in the People's Republic of China', *Journal of Conflict Resolution*, vol. 35, no. 1, March.

Peer

Baginsky, W. (2004) *Peer Mediation in the UK; A Guide for Schools*, <http:// www.creducation.org/resources/peermediationintheuk.pdf >

Hope, C. (2009) 'Peer mediation in schools', in E. Malcolm and F. O'Donnell (eds), *A Guide to Mediating in Scotland* (Dundee: Dundee University Press), pp. 111–12.

Planning

Rozee, L. and K. Powell (2010) *Mediation in Planning*, report commissioned by National Planning Forum and the Planning Inspectorate, <http://www. natplanforum.org.uk/Final%20Report%20-%20Mediation%20in%20 Planning%20-%20PDF.pdf>

Voluntary or mandatory

Ingleby, R. (1993) 'Court sponsored mediation: the case against mandatory participation', *56 Modern Law Review* 441. [An Australian viewpoint.]

Randolph, P. (2010) 'Compulsory mediation?', *New Law Journal*, April, vol. 60, issue 7,411, <http://www.newlawjournal.co.uk/nlj/content/litigation-v-mediation>

Reuben, R. (2007) 'Tort reform renews debate over mandatory mediation', *13 Dispute Resolution Magazine*, 2006–7, p. 13.

Sander, F. (2007) 'Another view of mandatory mediation', *13 Dispute Resolution Magazine*, 2006–7, p. 16.

Schmidt, M. (2013) 'Exploring the contradictions inherent in Court-ordered "voluntary" mediation', *Dispute Resolution Journal*, vol. 68, issue 1, pp. 103–16.

Tjersland, O., W. Gulbrandsen and H. Haavind (2015) 'Mandatory mediation outside the court – a process and effect study', *Conflict Resolution Quarterly*, vol. 33, no. 1, pp. 19–34. [Poor outcomes of mandatory mediation for divorcing couples in Norway.]

Working with clients

Aaron, M. and D. Hoffer (2007) 'Decision analysis as a method of evaluating the trial alternative', in S. Goldberg and others, *Dispute Resolution: Negotiation, Mediation, and Other Processes* (Austin: Wolters Kluwer).

Clark, B. (2006) *ADR and Scottish Commercial Litigators: A Study of Attitudes and Experience*, <http://ssrn.com/abstract=1002991>

Middleton-Smith, C. (2009) 'Mediation advocacy: hopes or expectations?', *The Mediator Magazine*, <http://www.squirepattonboggs.com/~/media/ files/insights/publications/2009/01/mediation-advocacy--hopes-and

-expectations/files/mediation-advocacy--hopes-and-expectations/
fileattachment/mediationadvocacyjan2009.pdf>

Nahrstadt, B. C. (2016) 'The defense perspective on mediation', *Defense Counsel Journal*, January, vol. 83, issue 1, pp. 68–83. [Practical advice to lawyers from an American defense attorney.]

Pel, M. (2008) *Referral to Mediation* (Sdu Uitgevers). [A really useful text, but hard to find and expensive as it's printed in The Netherlands. While it focuses mainly on referrals, there are interesting parts about preparation.]

Rushton, M., 'Effective mediation advocacy'. [Originally published in *The Mediator Magazine*, which is no longer available. However, Rushton has plans to make it available online so it would be worth looking for it using a search engine.]

Trevor, D. (2000) 'The more things change: why "alternative" dispute resolution still requires good old-fashioned lawyering', *Journal of Alternative Dispute Resolution in Employment*, vol. 2, issue 4, Winter, pp. 54–63.

Vickery, G. (1998) 'Seven principles for successfully advising a party in mediation', *ADR Bulletin*, vol. 1, no. 6, pp. 1–3, <http://epublications.bond. edu.au/adr/vol1/iss6/2/> [A brief paper with short descriptions of the principles which the author regards as key.]

Wade, J. (2004) 'Representing clients effectively in negotiation, conciliation and mediation', *Dispute Resolution Centre Resources* (Bond University), <http://epublications.bond.edu.au/drc_pubs/3> [An easy read, and practical.]

Wade, J. (2004) *Systematic Risk Analysis for Negotiators and Litigators: How to Help Clients Make Better Decisions*, Dispute Resolution Centre Resources (Bond University), <http://epublications.bond.edu.au/drc_pubs/2/> [A detailed approach to risk analysis.]

Wissler, R. L. (2010) 'Representation in mediation: what we know from empirical research', *Fordham Urban Law Journal*, vol. 37, pp. 419–71. Available at <http://papers.ssrn.com/sol3/papers.cfm?abstract_id=1710209&http:// papers.ssrn.com/sol3/papers.cfm?abstract_id=1710209##>

Case law

Aird and another v Prime Meridian Ltd [2006] EWCA Civ 1866

Bristow v The Princess Alexandra Hospital NHS Trust [2015] EWHC B22

Daniels v Metropolitan Police [2005] All ER (D) 225

Faidi and Another v Elliot Corporation [2012] EWCA Civ 287

Farm Assist Limited (in liquidation) v The Secretary of State for Environment, Food and Rural affairs (No. 2) 2009 EWHC 1102 (TCC)

FJM v CGM [2015] CSOH 130

Garritt-Critchley and Others v *Ronnan and Another [2014] EWHC 1774 (Ch)*
Halsey v *Milton Keynes General NHS Trust [2004] EWCA Civ 576*
James Carleton Seventh Earl of Malmesbury and others v *Strutt & Parker (a partnership) [2008] EWHC 424 (QB)*
Oceanbulk Shipping and Trading SA v *TMT Asia Ltd and others [2010] UKSC 44*
Oliver and Another v *Symons and Another [2012] EWCA Civ 267*
O'Neill v *Mermaid Touring Inc, 2013 U.S. Dist. LEXIS 129750, 1–2 (S.D.N.Y. Sept 10, 2013)*
PGF II SA v *OMFS Company 1 Ltd [2013] EWCA Civ 1288*
Reid v *Buckinghamshire Healthcare NHS Trust [2015] Lexis Citation 293*
Ryan v *Walls Construction Ltd – [2015] IECA 214*
Union Carbide Canada Inc. v *Bombardier Inc. [2014] S.C.J. No. 35*
Wu Yim Kwong Kingwind v *Manhood Development DCCJ 3839/2012)*

Directives, Green Papers and Rules

Directive 2008/52/EC of the European Parliament and of the Council of 21 May 2008 on certain aspects of mediation in civil and commercial matters.
Directive 2013/11/EU of the European Parliament and of the Council of 21 May 2013 on alternative dispute resolution for consumer disputes.
Green Paper on alternative dispute resolution in civil and commercial law, Brussels, 19.04.2002, COM (2002) 196 final.
Legal Ombudsman Scheme Rules (2015), <http://www.legalombudsman.org.uk/downloads/documents/publications/Scheme-Rules.pdf>

Legislation

Civil Evidence (Family Mediation) (Scotland) Act 1995
Civil Liability and Courts Act 2004
Cross-Border Mediation (Scotland) Regulations 2011
Education (Additional Support for Learning) (Scotland) Act 2004
Legal Aid, Sentencing & Punishment of Offenders Act 2012
Patient Rights (Scotland) Act 2011

Useful websites

(All these were accessed in May 2016)

Mediation provider

www.mediationscotland.com – commercial and workplace mediation.

Community mediation

www.gov.uk – A government resource with basic information and contact
points for assistance in Scotland, England and Wales. Type 'mediation'
into the search box to be directed to the various options.

www.gov.uk/how-to-resolve-neighbour-disputes/use-a-mediation-service –
England and Wales.

www.mediationnorthernireland.org – Northern Ireland.

www.sacro.org.uk – Scotland.

www.scmc.sacro.org.uk – Scottish Community Mediation Centre.

Family mediation

www.calmscotland.co.uk – Launched February 2016.

www.cyrenians.org.uk – Amber.

www.familymediationni.org.uk – Northern Ireland.

www.nfm.org.uk – England and Wales.

www.relationships-scotland.org.uk

General

www.ama.asn.au – Australian Mediation Association.

www.americanbar.org – American Bar Association.

www.civilmediation.org – The Civil Mediation Council is the 'recognised
authority for England and Wales for civil, commercial, workplace and
other non-family mediation'.

www.cpradr.org – The website of the US-based International Institute
for Conflict Prevention and Resolution shows some examples of
model dispute resolution clauses to include in commercial contracts.
Such clauses have the obvious benefit of ensuring that, if a dispute
does arise, the parties have already agreed the initial path towards
resolution.

www.eur-lex.europa.eu – Access to European Union Law.

www.imimediation.org – The International Mediation Institute, based in The
Hague, seeks to bring high standards of competency into the mediation
profession.

www.lawsociety.com.au – The Law Society of New South Wales, Australia.

www.mediate.com – A US-based publication providing articles about current mediation issues.

www.qls.com.au – Queensland Law Society, Australia.

www.scottishlegalcomplaints.org.uk – Scottish Legal Complaints Commission.

www.scottishmediation.org.uk – Scottish Mediation Network is the umbrella organisation for mediation in Scotland.

www.mediation.com.sg – Singapore Mediation Centre.

www.simc.com.sg – Singapore International Mediation Centre.

www.simi.org.sg – Singapore International Mediation Institute.

www.sidra.academy – Singapore International Dispute Resolution Academy.

www.themii.ie – The Mediators' Institute of Ireland.

www.virtualmediationlab.com – Virtual Mediation Lab. <www.youtube.com/watch?v=xTbj-eHwX-w> A condensed version of a mediation, for which you will need a speedy internet connection.

<https://www.youtube.com/watch?v=-neknWYzd8o> Simulation of an online mediation with the author as mediator in Scotland, and the parties in Brazil and Israel.

Peer mediation

www.peermediationnetwork.org.uk

INDEX